We Are the Church Together

We Are the Church Together

Cultural Diversity
in Congregational Life

CHARLES R. FOSTER
THEODORE BRELSFORD

TRINITY PRESS INTERNATIONAL
VALLEY FORGE, PENNSYLVANIA

Trinity Press International, P.O. Box 851, Valley Forge, PA 19482-0851

Library of Congress Cataloging-in-Publication Data

Foster, Charles R., 1937-
    We are the church together : cultural diversity in congregational life / Charles R. Foster, Theodore Brelsford.
      p.   cm.
    Includes bibliographical references and index.
    ISBN 1-56338-169-9 (pbk. : alk. paper)
    1. Mutliculturalism—Religious aspects—Christianity. 2. Pastoral theology. 3. United States—Church history—20th century.
I. Brelsford, Theodore. II. Title.
BR115.C8F635   1996
250—dc20
                                    96-12885
                                      CIP

Ediset by Joan Marie Laflamme

Printed in the United States of America

96 97 98 99 00 01 02 7 6 5 4 3 2 1

With appreciation to the members of
Cedar Grove United Methodist Church,
Oakhurst Presbyterian Church,
and
Northwoods United Methodist Church
for their hospitality,
the courage of their vision,
and the vibrancy of their life together.

91163

Contents

We Are the Church Together

Introduction

> I am the church!
> You are the church!
> We are the church together!
> All who follow Jesus, all around the world!
> Yes, we are the church together![1]

Children in Sunday school classes across the nation often stand in a circle to sing the hymn "We Are the Church." While singing the first line, "I am the church," they point to themselves. When they reach the line "You are the church," they point to someone else in the circle. As they sing "We are the church together," they sweep their hands in a large circle to include everyone present. Most children sing this song with children who share their racial, ethnic, and class heritage and experience. The image of church conveyed by their singing is locally homogenous and globally inclusive. When children sing the song in congregations that embrace racial, ethnic, and/or class differences as integral to their identities as Christian faith communities, the image of church is radically altered. These differences exist *in the congregation* as well as *all around the world.* In many respects their experience of racial, ethnic, and/or class *togetherness* challenges traditional notions of church for many Protestant Christians in the United States and Canada.

One of the great struggles for Jews and Christians through the ages has been their relationship to "the other"—those different from themselves. One of the first stories in Genesis explores the tensions between nomadic and agrarian cultures. Early Hebrew codes focused on ways to receive strangers—even enemies—who approached their homes. Guidelines for hospitality, codes of conduct for war, all ethical principles of neighborliness emerged from their experience of struggling for ways to respond to the differences they encountered in others.

The markers of difference attracting people's attention of people have varied through the ages. Differences grounded in gender may

1

be the most persistent and pervasive, but class, ethnicity, race, religion, language, family lineage, nationality, and cultural heritage and practices have all been emphasized in distinguishing one group of people from another. The way groups of people distinguish and make sense of these differences contributes to a politic of difference. Through the ages that politic has tended to focus on the creation of *insiders* (those like us) and *outsiders* (those different from us).

A major shift in the way people in the United States approach the presence of difference in human experience is taking place. The shift is evident in the attention given to revising social theories and altering social policies to enhance the civil rights of people oppressed primarily on the basis of their difference from those in power. Living in the midst of this shift involves a change of consciousness for those who have been both historically insiders and outsiders.

A grant from the Lilly Endowment, Inc., to Candler School of Theology of Emory University for the study of congregations provided an opportunity to explore the dynamics of difference in three historically mainline Protestant congregations located in Atlanta, Georgia. These congregations have embraced racial and cultural difference as integral to their identity as communities of faith. By that decision they stand over against the cultural, racial, and class enclaves predominant in the gathering of Christians into faith communities not only in Atlanta but throughout the nation.

A research project designed to study the dynamics of diversity in congregational life could have focused on a range of issues and questions. Our research interests, however, have sought over the years to illumine the relationship of education and religion in communities of faith and their social contexts.[2] Working as part of a research team of six persons, we spent a year in these congregations attempting to discern how their members view themselves to be church and how they order their lives to incorporate children, youth, and newcomers into the commitments and practices integral to that view. Our attention, in other words, focused in theoretical terms on the relationship of ecclesiology and education.

Since our own approach to the study of these issues has drawn primarily on historical, theological, and philosophical methodologies, we immediately immersed ourselves in the rich body of literature known as *congregational studies*. The work of James Hopewell challenged us to look beyond the "creeds, governing structures, and programs" for the "symbols and signals of the world . . . gathered and grounded" in the congregation's own "idiom." The *Handbook for Congregational Studies* introduced us to the rich range of methodologies for the study of congregational identity, the context of the congregation, and its processes and programs. The works of Nancy Ammerman, Stephen Warner, and others provided models and guidelines for our own efforts.[3]

This book grows out of that study. In the first chapter we seek to situate the quest in these congregations to embrace difference in social, religious, and historical context as well as the implications to be found from this discussion for our research methodology. Chapters 2, 3, and 4 tell stories of the dynamics of difference in these three Atlanta-area congregations: Cedar Grove United Methodist, Oakhurst Presbyterian, and Northwoods United Methodist Churches. In chapter 5 we examine the impact of a commitment to difference on the view of church in these three congregations. In chapter 6 our attention is directed to the persistent educational task these congregations face in forming community life that embodies a vision of church embracing difference. In the last chapter we explore new practices of faith and knowing emerging from the congregational embrace of difference as integral to their identities as communities of faith.

We began our research wondering what might lead people from diverse racial, cultural, and in some cases economic backgrounds to gather together as faith communities when most other historically mainline Protestant churches separate themselves along those lines. As we settled into our study, we became increasingly fascinated with the contrast between the fragility of their institutional life and the vibrancy of their fellowship, worship, and mission. We had some awareness they might illumine possibilities for the increasing encounters among diverse peoples occurring in United States society prompted by changes in immigration laws, heightened social mobility, and the consequences of civil rights and affirmative action legislation following the Brown *vs.* Topeka school desegregation suit in 1954.

Our own interest in exploring their ways of dealing with difference also points to the pervasiveness of a shift in the national consciousness about the meanings and practices integral to what we are calling the dynamics of difference. Our perception that the dynamics of difference need not be threatening but instead might contribute to enriched views and practices of community reflects the extent of our own responsiveness to creative possibilities emerging from the changing dynamics of difference in the country. That emerging consciousness provided the impetus for this study and influenced the course of our research.

FOSTER'S EMERGING CONSCIOUSNESS OF DIFFERENCE

The study of diversity in congregational life grows out of a long and deep interest I have had in understanding what happens when cultures encounter each other. I first became conscious of hierarchical dynamics in the social and political relationships of peoples from different cultures in stories my father told. Many were based on conversations with Japanese-American farmers during his rounds as a county agricultural extension agent in my home community in the years immediately after World War II. He talked about young men who had been recruited into the army even as the government forcibly deported their families to internment camps in the desert interior of the nation. He told about soldiers, recognized nationally for their bravery in some of the toughest fighting on the European front lines, whose names had been removed from the community honor roll. He described the experience some had in returning to homes and farms maintained by caring neighbors. But he also related the experience of others who returned to discover their neighbors had appropriated their crops or confiscated their property.

The stories my father told burned the reality of oppression and marginalization in the experience of some people into my consciousness. Those stories increasingly affected the way I, as an heir to the heritage of white Anglo-Saxon Protestants, saw the relationships of Native Americans to the fur traders, explorers, settlers, and military forces of the United States, Great Britain, and France in other stories my father told and in the books I read as an adolescent. Chief Joseph, Crazy Horse, and Sitting Bull became tragic heroes in my expanding world view. The reality of the pain of oppressed peoples was heightened as I later became aware of the struggles Harriet Tubman, Mary McLeod Bethune, Nat Turner, Booker T. Washington, and Washington Carver had with the evils of slavery and segregation.

I did not recognize my own participation in the racial and ethnic cultural power dynamics of the church and nation, however, until many years later, when I became increasingly conscious of the cultural bias in my teaching. I discovered my assumptions about how persons learn, classroom organization, and the criteria for evaluating student work often hindered the learning of students whose assumptions had been formed in ethnic cultural traditions different from my own. The dynamics of power I had established in the classroom always required some students to choose between the cultural assumptions I imposed on their learning and the cultural assumptions that connected them to their communities of origin.[4] I discovered that the oppression experienced by Japanese-American farmers in the community in which I grew up was, in many ways, similar to the oppression I created for students who did not know how to negotiate the differences in our cultural assumptions about what and how to learn. That insight helped me to begin the long journey of consciousness into the depths of the collusion of white folks in the United States to the marginalization and suffering of many of the nation's minorities—especially those who because of skin color could not "pass" or assimilate into the dominant cultural experience.

Clarence Joseph Rivers, who helped introduce the idiom of African-American music into Roman Catholic liturgy, provided me with an early clue to the content of the power dynamics in worship and educational settings that included people from diverse racial and ethnic cultural backgrounds. He contrasted the ocular traditions of the West with the oral traditions of Africa. The former, Rivers wrote, "tends to comprehend the world through the bias of the sense of sight, a bias that arises out of a book-oriented culture, a culture in which sight dominates and mutes the other senses." The eye focuses on one thing at a time, favors "continuity, lineality, and connectedness." These characteristics enhance the human capacity to analyze, to "separate conceptually things that in reality are not separate," and to distinguish oneself from the object of one's knowing. They establish learning environments conducive to the formation of scientific, economic, and political institutions, which have influenced the course of Western societies for several centuries.

Cultures that emphasize oral traditions for communicating and relating, Rivers continued, comprehend the world through the interdependence of the senses so that "touch and smell and hearing" are on an "equal plane with seeing," leading to the involvement of the whole body in activities such as worship and learning. Consequently, engagement rather than detachment is valued among the learning responses of students deeply rooted in oral traditions of learning.[5] Participation is encouraged. Consciousness of the interdependence of the parts of the whole is valued. I now consider Rivers's dichotomy between oral and ocular learning styles to be a little too neat. Many people of European heritage rely on touch, smell, and hearing in their approaches to learning, and many persons of African descent value the linearity integral to reading. Rivers, however, first made me aware of the influence of culture on the ways people learn.

I subsequently encountered in the work of the anthropologist Edward T. Hall new insights into the complexity of human interaction in the meeting of cultures. His research findings convinced me that the difficulties United States politicians and business leaders (and church leaders and educators, as well) had in other countries and cultures could be traced to their overwhelming ignorance of the non-verbal patterns of communication they encountered. Hall traced these patterns (which in turn frame verbal communication) back into human prehistory. Cultural approaches to the meaning of such things as space, time, subsistence, learning, defense, and sexuality deeply rooted in biological activities took distinctive forms through the ages in different cultural groups. Since these patterns are for the most part only implicitly acknowledged, their differences become stumbling blocks to peoples encountering each other—even in the most basic of human activities such as establishing a time for a meeting or deciding what to eat.[6] They also inspire political strategies designed to overcome the frustrations people experience when they encounter cultural differences in the classroom, political or economic negotiations, or administration of some group or organization, by diminishing or destroying the impact of those differences. Reliance on the exercise of power in these efforts for the most part only enhances the potential for oppression, suffering, marginalization, and pain for those engaged in the encounter.

My initial quest to understand the political dynamics in the encounters of people from diverse racial and cultural heritages was historical. As a religious educator, I wondered how churches had used education among peoples who did not share their dominant cultural assumptions and values. It was a sobering quest. I discovered that churches in the United States had adapted specific educational strategies to different cultural groups based on the shared perceptions of church leaders about their potential for being assimilated into the dominant racial and ethnic culture of the church and nation. In other words, the education sponsored by the churches furthered the dominant cultural assumptions about the relative value of the place and contribution of diverse races and ethnic cultural traditions to the nation, and by implication to the churches of the dominant culture as well.[7] These insights heightened my interest in the possibility of studying congregations whose embrace of diversity challenges these hegemonic patterns of the past. They also intensified my awareness of the difficulty these congregations face in seeking to alter the prevailing patterns for dealing with difference in contemporary church life in the United States.

BRELSFORD'S EMERGING CONSCIOUSNESS
OF PLURALISM

My decision to engage in a study of cultural diversity in congregational life relates to my enduring interest in the impact on faith and identity of cross-cultural experience and the emergence of what may be termed pluralistic consciousness—a clear awareness and acceptance of the presence of irreducibly diverse cultures, traditions, and perspectives. The emergence of such consciousness in me seems to have begun when, at the age of nineteen, I spent a summer traveling in Western Europe with two friends. This travel venture was unprecedented in my immediate family. My parents were, and are, frugal people. Neither had attended college or traveled extensively even within the United States. Yet, they somehow gave me a love for education and exploration. There were stories of my paternal grandfather traveling to California as a young man. I had heard my mother, and her mother, praise the ways in which reading can "take us places we could not otherwise go." I found encouragement and support as I worked for a year after high school, while I planned to travel abroad and then begin college.

That summer of travel turned out to be a crucial part of my education. We began in Germany, the home of my maternal ancestors, and toured throughout Western Europe. One friend had family in Switzerland who provided us a comfortable "home base." Still, we were foreigners. I had the feeling of visiting different "worlds"[8] as we moved from country to country, city to city, countryside to seaside—worlds very different from the one I knew at home in rural Pennsylvania. As a tourist I learned something of local customs and perspectives. We worked hard to find restaurants with a local clientele, often conversing with garbage collectors, carpenters, or painters for clues. We stayed at small out-of-the-way hostels and inns. We took time in each new place to "hang out" and observe and participate in the local culture. Even as these new worlds enriched and became part of my world view, they remained foreign to me. I never felt fully at home in them. But I returned home and then went to college at the end of that summer knowing something about the meanings of culture. Perhaps most important, I knew for the first time that I had one. I realized I lived in and was shaped by a particular culture.

A few years later, shortly after a second trip to Europe and a semester's study in Salzburg, Austria, I went to a small restaurant in rural Pennsylvania with my brother. I looked around in fascination, seeing it with new eyes. It was as exotic to me as a cafe on some cobblestone street in Italy or a Munich beer garden. There were local customs, a local dialect, local food. There was also a blissful at-homeness here, just as in small towns in Europe—people resting comfortably in long-standing local traditions. The customers in this small-town diner knew the language and customs and expectations. They knew each other and themselves. Their roles seemed clear. They served and ate food. They conversed in "plain English." They interacted in the accepted local fashion, seemingly without awareness of the existence of a local fashion. They did not seem entirely unaware of other possibilities—other scripts or patterns of being and relating—but they seemed happily unconcerned with any such alternatives.

I sensed I would never again be quite so comfortable or so "at home." This is the nature of cross-cultural experience and perhaps all of education—one's world becomes broader, and more complex. That which was strange becomes a bit more familiar, and that which was familiar becomes a bit more strange.

My sense of the impact of culture on how we see ourselves and our world grew through my college years and into seminary. I came to understand that assumptions such as individual selfhood and the linear and progressive nature of time are particularly Western. Some other cultures see self-identity as communal and time as cyclical. I also saw, for example, that if we were of Italian rather than of German and English descent, my father and I would think nothing of hugging and kissing one another. Likewise, our perceptions of physical and social phenomena are affected by our cultural habits—our habits of seeing and making sense. My study of psychology, philosophy, sociology, and quantum physics led me to believe that what we see is very much influenced by what we expect to see, how we are trained to look, or the categories we have for processing our perceptions.

I began to struggle personally with the difficulty of how to sustain a meaningful identity in a particular tradition in the face of my awareness and honoring of a plurality of traditions. Clifford Geertz focused the dilemma for me in his discussion of the role of religion in culture. Geertz argues that persons need to hold their orienting beliefs as absolutely true and universally valid, and that cultural myths and practices serve to underwrite such beliefs. But anyone familiar with the incommensurability among cultures will see that no set of orienting beliefs is universal. Rather, beliefs *are* culturally formed and sustained, and to the degree they are sustained, they "function" within the culture to make the world meaningful. The dilemma Geertz sets up but does not fully address is that once one perceives that beliefs are always *only* functional, one can no longer hold them to be universal. But if one cannot hold beliefs to be universal, then they cannot function to orient the person in the world.

I experienced this dilemma personally. I was aware that the traditions of my German and English heritage, my rural Pennsylvania community, and my conservative Protestant Christianity were not universal. They did not constitute *the* world, but *a* world—a particular way of being and putting one's being in meaningful context. This way of being in context—this world as imagined—functioned well for my family, community, and church. But, as Geertz argues, it functions because the members of those groups take it to be absolutely valid—"just plain common sense," "the way things are." They take it for granted, for example that men are supposed to be the providers and heads of their household; people should shake hands upon meeting; trees do not have souls; God is manifest as Father, Son, and Holy Spirit; and human beings were created by God and did not evolve.

This world view had ceased to function for me, because I no longer saw it as universal or absolute. Rather, I saw it as stipulative and functional. I saw these beliefs, and all beliefs or habits of thinking and seeing, as ordering personal and social experience, not as naming reality. I saw other functional options. Women might head or share leadership for households as well as men; some people (cultures) kiss upon greeting and find a handshake strange or rude; some people (cultures) assume trees have souls or spirits with which humans can and should communicate (and this belief tends to discourage ruthless deforestation); millions of good religious people (especially in Asia) do not experience God as Father, Son, and Holy Spirit; and I myself had come to accept an evolutionary/developmental understanding of human origins and human life.

As I became increasingly aware of the functional character of any view I considered or adopted, I held it as relative, stipulative, and not absolute. Geertz points out, however, that if it were not absolute, it would not, in fact, function for me. The beliefs in the view would not do their ordering work if I did not really believe in their unquestionable validity. How can one have a functional world as imagined if one imagines that one is only imagining it? I discovered I was not alone in this crisis of belief. Peter Berger, Robert Bellah, and Robert MacAfee Brown, for example, speak to the fairly new and widespread dilemma of "choosing" one's beliefs and then "believing" in them.[9]

I began to think of this Geertzian quandary as a postmodern dilemma. And I began to think of cultural diversity and cross-cultural experience as precipitating this dilemma. It is no longer the case that one group, person, or theory can be set up as the centering norm around which all else is to be defined—the modernist propensity toward hegemony. Easy, unquestioned, at-homeness is increasingly difficult for growing numbers of us. As many have documented, the astounding advances in travel and communications technology in the twentieth century have created a global neighborhood; we cannot ignore or avoid "the other." The world has become pluralistic for us, and we are still struggling to cope with this development. Kenneth Gergen's *The Saturated Self* makes particularly clear the impact of technological change on our self-understanding. As Gergen puts it, "Beliefs in the true and the good depend on a reliable homogeneous group of supporters, who define what is reliably 'there,' plain and simple." But such "reliable homogeneity" is gone or fading. Large numbers of people live in multiple places and cultural contexts during their lifetimes, far from their places and cultures of birth. At the same time, communications technologies bring diverse peoples from around the nation and around the globe into our homes every day.[10]

I knew when I began this study that some contemporary philosophers were also wrestling with the impact of cultural pluralism on our notions of truth.[11] What happens when we are forced or decide to take the divergent views of others seriously? What happens when others' perspectives of the world and of us become part of our own perceptions? What happens when these new and varying perspectives continually multiply? How do we sustain confidence in our particular views in the face of proliferating viable alternatives? Or should we? Do we need a deeply trusted world as imagined? Or can we live with multiple worlds or a loosely held world?

My interest in cultural diversity in congregational life grows out of these more general personal and philosophical interests in the psycho-social effects and implications of the increasingly unavoidable experiences of a more or less continuously expanding world view. At the outset I saw these culturally diverse communities boldly living into this dimension of contemporary (postmodern) life. I came to this study looking for clues about how to embrace the integrity of one's own perspective while also respecting the integrity of divergent perspectives. I wondered whether persons in culturally diverse congregations might come to understand or live their religious faith in some distinctive ways in comparison to members of more homogenous faith communities. I suspected that embracing cultural diversity would both expand and destabilize a person's understanding of his or her world. I also believed that culture and religion are not distinctively separable—might embracing cultural diversity lead to embracing religious or theological diversity? I expected to see cross-cultural negotiations around such culture-laden practices as music, eating, liturgy. And, since "ritual generates the conviction that religious conceptions are veridical,"[12] I expected to see persons in these congregations wrestling (probably subconsciously) with epistemological issues: If I acknowledge that my beliefs are culturally formed and are among a wide array of alternative and, in some cases, opposing beliefs, how do I "know" that my beliefs are true? How do we as a community remain open to "others" and yet also preserve and perpetuate "ourselves"—our wisdom, values, and knowledge? Might there be hints in these congregations about the nature of faith, knowledge, and education in a pluralistic society? These are some of the questions and predispositions I brought to this study.

THE STORY OF THE RESEARCH PROJECT

A grant from the Lilly Endowment, Inc., to Candler School of Theology of Emory University to study congregations provided us with an opportunity to move beyond these historical and philosophical inquiries to an exploration of the ways ethnic and racial diversity functions in congregations that embrace those differences as gifts to be celebrated rather than as problems to be solved. A sabbatical year from teaching and administrative responsibilities at Candler School of Theology made the project appear, on the surface at least, to be feasible for Foster. The congregational studies project directed by Thomas Frank, Director of the Rollins Center at Candler and Associate Professor of Church Administration, provided a larger framework for the development and reflection on our research efforts. The questions and insights of faculty colleagues—Thomas Frank, Pamela Couture, Robert Franklin, Gail O'Day, Sally Purvis, Don Saliers, and James Fowler—during a series of monthly seminars proved to be invaluable in raising pointed questions, clarifying issues, and illuminating implications from our research efforts.

The research team included Foster and Brelsford as well as Vivian Green, Merry Porter, Amy Stanley, and Lorine Tevi, master's degree candidates at Candler. We became full partners in the research phase of the project. Our varied sensitivities, commitments, and cultural perspectives helped shape the research agenda and illuminate our conclusions. The task of preparing the research reports and the manuscript for publication has been taken up by Foster and Brelsford. This work is the product of our joint efforts. We planned the work together and collaborated on the introduction and conclusion and chapter 2. Brelsford wrote chapters 3 and 7, and Foster the rest. We revised and edited the whole volume together.

As a research team, we discovered in the formation of our research efforts a microcosm of the dynamics to be found in the churches we studied. We included four women and two men and represented African-American, European-American and Fijian perspectives on church life and faith. Encountering the differences in our own perceptions rooted in the differences of our cultural experiences significantly enhanced our conversations about the meanings of the things we saw and heard in the three congregations we studied during the 1991-92 academic year. Our work has been significantly enriched by the insights of colleagues who have served as consultants to the project at one point or another during its research and writing phases: Nancy Ammerman, Rebecca Chopp, James Fowler, Thomas Frank, Grant Shockley, Luther Smith, and Thomas Thangaraj of Candler School of Theology; Margaret Spencer from Emory University; Anne Wimberly from the Interdenominational Theological Center; Mary Elizabeth Moore from the School of Theology at Claremont; David Ng from San Francisco Theological Seminary; and Christelle Estrada from the Pasadena, California, public school district. We are especially indebted to Craig Dykstra and James P. Wind from the Lilly Endowment, Inc. for their vision for the study of congregations, interest in issues of diversity in churches, and commitment to the personal as well as financial support for the project. Our faculty secretary, Brenda Stevenson, ably assisted us in readying the manuscript for publication.

The hospitality and generosity of the Cedar Grove United Methodist Church, Oakhurst Presbyterian Church, and Northwoods United Methodist Church in the larger Atlanta, Georgia, metropolitan area enhanced our investment and energy in their lives and mission. We are grateful to their pastoral leadership—Martha Forrest, Gibson Stroupe, Caroline Leach, Jerome Hamm, and Winston Worrell, and the lay leaders and committee members in each congregation who provided guidance and assistance in this research project: Sam and Glenda Butler, DuRhonda Davenport, Eileen Dodson, Joe Dobbs, Shirley Everett, William Gray, Roy Hatcher, Jackie Johnson,

Merilyn Kagelmacher, Seymour Nelms, and Earl White in the Cedar Grove Church; Inez Fleming, Wanda White and members of Oakhurst's Session, and Lamar Carter, Don Lacey, Beverly Rhodes, and Dorrit Stephens and the Administrative Council at Northwoods. We especially appreciate the willingness of every member in the three congregations who took time to talk to us. They gave direction to our studies, risked some of their most cherished values and commitments to our scrutiny with unbelievable graciousness, and some among them reviewed and critiqued what we wrote about them. These congregations were not only the subjects of our inquiry, but we were the recipients of their hospitality. It is to the story of our encounter with diversity through these congregations and the meanings that their experience might have for other churches and institutions as they seek to understand and respond to the intensification of the pluralism in the nation and world that we now turn.

Notes

1. Richard K. Avery and Donald S. Marsh, "We Are the Church," in *The United Methodist Hymnal*, ed. Carlton R. Young (Nashville: The United Methodist Publishing House, 1989), 558.

2. See Jack L. Seymour, Robert T. O'Gorman, and Charles R. Foster, *The Church in the Education of the Public* (Nashville: Abingdon Press, 1984); Charles R. Foster, *Ethnicity in the Education of the Church* (Nashville: Scarritt Press, 1987).

3. James F. Hopewell, *Congregation: Stories and Structures*, ed. Barbara G. Wheeler (Philadelphia: Fortress Press, 1987), 5; Jackson W. Carroll, Carl S. Dudley, and William McKinney, *Handbook for Congregational Studies* (Nashville: Abingdon Press, 1986); Nancy Tatom Ammerman, *Bible Believers: Fundamentalists in the Modern World* (New Brunswick: Rutgers University Press, 1987); Stephen R. Warner, *New Wine in Old Wineskins: Evangelicals and Liberals in a Small-town Church* (Berkeley: University of California Press, 1988). For an extensive overview of the field, its literature, and research methodologies, see James P. Wind and James W. Lewis, *American Congregations* (Chicago: University of Chicago Press, 1994), a two-volume work.

4. I am indebted to Fumitaka Matsuoka for his discussion of the power dynamics in intercultural communication in "Pluralism at Home: Globalization within North America," *Theological Education* 26 (Spring 1990), Supplement 1: 39-40.

5. Clarence Joseph Rivers, "The Oral African Tradition Versus the Ocular Western Tradition," *This Far by Faith: American Black Worship and Its*

African Roots (Washington, D.C.: The National Office for Black Catholics and the Liturgical Conference, 1977), 41-42, 46.

6. Edward T. Hall, *The Silent Language* (Greenwich, CT: Fawcett Publications, Inc., 1959), 44-45.

7. For an extended discussion of these patterns in the education of the church, see Charles R. Foster, "Imperialism in the Education of the Church," *Religious Education* 86 (Winter 1991): 145-56.

8. I am using *world* here in the psycho-mythico sense of the wholeness of one's context—what the Greeks called cosmos and Clifford Geertz calls "the world as imagined" (Clifford Geertz, *The Interpretation of Cultures* [New York: Basic Books, Inc., Publishers, 1973]). By saying I visited "different worlds" I mean I encountered other cultures and persons who, as evidenced by their actions and their words, imagined the world differently from the way I did.

9. Peter Berger, *The Heretical Imperative: Contemporary Possibilities of Religious Affirmation* (Garden City, NY: Anchor Press, 1979); Robert N. Bellah, *Beyond Belief: Essays on Religion in a Post-Traditional World* (New York: Harper & Row, Publishers, 1970); Robert MacAfee Brown, *Is Faith Obsolete?* (Philadelphia: Westminster Press, 1974).

10. Kenneth J. Gergen, *The Saturated Self: Dilemmas of Identity in Contemporary Life* (New York: Basic Books, 1991), xi.

11. See, for example, Richard Rorty, *Objectivity, Relativism, and Truth: Philosophical Papers Volume I* (Cambridge: Cambridge University Press, 1991); and Richard J. Bernstein, *Beyond Objectivism and Relativism: Science, Hermeneutics, and Praxis* (Philadelphia: University of Pennsylvania Press, 1985).

12. Geertz, 112.

1

CELEBRATING DIFFERENCE

INTRODUCTION

I grew up in the Baptist church (but became inactive as an adult). When my brother and his wife had a child . . . we began talking about where we got our values . . . and it was the church. So we started to identify the kind of church we thought a child should be brought up in . . . and of all the criteria . . . the first . . . was that it be multicultural. The denomination was not in the criteria at all. . . . My brother (had heard about this church) and we joined. It was exactly what we wanted because of the support and the strength that one gets from diversity and it was genuinely diverse rather than people trying to become like one another; it was a celebration of the differences.

—European-American woman

Many people, both within and outside organized religion, are concerned about the current religious and spiritual climate of the nation. Journalists, scholars, commentators, religionists— all write about how the religious scene is in flux, but they hardly agree in their interpretation of what is happening.[1]

Most interpreters of the flux in the contemporary religious scene in the American United States focus their attention on the larger picture. Some describe the changing demography of declining memberships in historically Protestant mainline denominations and growing evangelical denominations and congregations. Some explore the implications in changing lifestyles and social perspectives on the ministries of the church. Others examine such things as the emerging challenge to dominant-culture spirituality and values from the rapidly growing Hispanic religious community in the nation or the sophisticated and publicity conscious megachurches.[2]

Some focus their attention on radical shifts in the relationship of individual and community and in the private and public roles of religious communities in the nation. Robert Bellah and his colleagues, for example, have examined the extent to which commitments originating in the nation's religious and republican heritage have "grown cancerous," unleashing in the process an excessive individualism threatening "the survival of freedom itself." Robert Wuthnow has probed the "growing struggle" for the nation's soul in the competition between religious conservatives and liberals over the relationship between religious convictions and public behavior. Wade Clark Roof and William McKinney have examined the influence of an "enhanced religious individualism" on the new assumption among many people in the nation that religion is itself a matter of choice. Roof and McKinney locate the sources to shifts such as these attitudes toward religion in the intense "search for spirituality and inner truth" originating in the "youth counterculture of the 1960s" and the "evangelical revival of the mid-to-late 1970s."[3] The impetus to each of these works may be found in the attention of researchers to the shattering of old perspectives and structures, the privatization of religious sensibilities and habits, and the increasing difficulty among historically mainline religious communities to relate to the spiritual quests of people at the end of the twentieth century.

Amazingly little attention has been given to the influence of the Civil Rights Movement (a movement corresponding in time to the youth counterculture and evangelical movements) on the religious sensibilities and practices among that group of denominations which make up the historically mainline churches living out of their European-American heritage.[4] The social vision of that movement galvanized church leaders to implement the intent of governmental civil-rights legislation in denominational policies and procedures. The vision of the Civil Rights Movement, with its religious roots, mobilized clergy and laity to work for racial and cultural equality in and outside church structures. It inspired church leaders to establish new criteria for the goals of church mission and the distribution of church funds. It altered the consciousness of denominational editors about the content of curriculum resources used in church schools. Denominations altered the composition of their staffs and elected officials to increase the representation of women, racial and ethnic minorities, and people with disabilities. And the Civil Rights Movement intensified the historical mainline commitment to public schools. The cost has been high. Funds have been withheld. People have withdrawn their membership. Bureaucracies have been restructured time and again as denominational leaders have tried to keep something of that social vision alive while responding to other demands on diminishing resources.

These struggles, however, have occurred primarily at the judicatory or national levels of church policy and program development. The commitment to a racially and ethnically inclusive church has yet to take form in policies and procedures directed to the local congregation. E. Allen Richardson's observation that the voluntary congregation is a "gathering of people of similar ethnic backgrounds and social rank" aptly characterizes most of the congregations that make up the traditional Christian Protestant mainstream.[5] To this day, most of the congregations in these denominations remain among the most segregated of contemporary institutions. Although denominational leaders decry the lack of racial and ethnic cultural integration at the local level, they have given little attention, funds, or time to the implementation of a culturally diverse vision of community in the congregation.

A NEW KIND OF COMMUNITY

Here and there across the country, however, isolated congregations embracing a vision of a racially and culturally pluralistic community stand over against the prevailing emphasis on racial, cultural, and linguistic homogeneity in congregational life.[6] The number of these congregations is increasing, giving the phenomenon something of the character of a grass-roots movement—an indigenous quest for racially and culturally diverse community. Drawing primarily on the inner resources of the congregation and its leaders (and occasionally with some financial assistance and encouragement from judicatory officials), these congregations look beyond Martin Luther King, Jr.'s, dream of a community where children of all races might study and play together to biblical visions of a community in which all languages, for example, are necessary for the adequate praise of God (see Acts 2).

No two of these culturally diverse congregations are alike. The history and values of the congregation, the racial and ethnic compo-

sition of the local community, and the theological vision and quest
for community among the clergy and laity who establish the course
of congregational life "localize" the character and mission in each
congregation. Local circumstances and setting further define the shape
of their stories. Historic patterns of relating among blacks and whites
in Atlanta, Georgia, provide a quite different challenge to the efforts
of a congregation to create community from a congregation in Los
Angeles with its history of European-American, Asian-American,
African-American and Mexican-American social and relational patterns.

Some congregations are like one in New Jersey, with members
drawn from all races and more than twenty-five nations. Its worship
follows, with few changes, the European liturgical, musical, and
homiletical traditions of the denomination. It uses denominational
educational resources designed for a predominantly European-American constituency in its Sunday school. Its administrative structure
follows denominational guidelines with little attention to cultural
patterns of leadership or decision-making. Although English is the
second language for most church members, all conversation, business, and worship are in English. People talk about the long time it
takes to make decisions to ensure that the diversity of perspectives in
the membership is taken into consideration. The cultural gifts of
church members are valued, but they are viewed as enriching rather
than transforming congregational perspectives and values. The congregation operates, in other words, from the assumption that its
immigrant members will be assimilated into the dominant cultural
values of the denomination and nation, with one significant excep-
tion. Race is *not* a stumbling block to full inclusion. This congregation *looks* different from those more homogenous congregations
down the street, but it *feels* similar.

A quite different perspective is evident in other culturally diverse
congregations to be found in historically mainline Protestant denominations. These congregations explicitly repudiate assimilationist strategies for dealing with racial and cultural difference. They strive
instead, through their mission statements and ways of living and
working together, to shift the power dynamics among the
congregation's racial and cultural groups from one of hierarchy and
dominance to one of interaction and mutuality. This task is not easy.
It requires long-term persistence to break through attitudes, habits,
and unconscious behaviors that sustain the hierarchy of cultures found
in the structures and practices of churches and other social institutions.

The shift in power relations gradually occurs as church members persevere in the tasks of mutually constructing a common experience, patching up inevitable breaks in communication, renewing shattered commitments, and re-examining familiar interpretations of ancient texts, which have sustained patterns of patriarchy and oppression in church life. Their efforts to form, sustain, and renew congregational life and mission in order to affirm cultural and racial diversity occur through a constant process of negotiating cultural perspectives and practices—even to the smallest details of worship, education, and mission. This process requires an increasing capacity for a mutual critique—becoming vulnerable, in other words, to building a common life that encompasses ways each constitutive group in the congregation perceives the others.[7] The resulting structural fragility in the voluntary commitments of members to each other has a liminal quality; it can easily be shattered. And yet, at the same time, it creates an openness to what Christians have historically called the movements of the Spirit. The capacity to trust in the gracefulness of an open-ended future has an eschatological dimension to it. Apprehension about the future of their common life, in other words, is often exceeded by anticipation of some new and profoundly transforming experience from the future. The effect may be seen in a tolerance for the ambiguity arising from the discoveries among culturally diverse peoples that they probably will never be able to understand or appreciate any *other* fully. This tolerance seems to move beyond an acceptance of diversity to a real celebration of differences.

These congregations are as varied as the communities in which they are located. A congregation near Hollywood, California, includes long-time European-American members, Salvadorans, Filipinos, gays and lesbians, and new, young European-American families mostly associated with the film industry. While visiting a meeting of the youth of the church, the young people (almost equally divided among Salvadorans, Filipinos, and European Americans) shared their plans to start a dance ministry in the neighborhood in an effort to keep youth from becoming involved in local gang activities. Another congregation, in Atlanta, with members drawn almost equally from African, African-American, Caribbean, and European-American constituencies, struggles with conflicting cultural assumptions and expectations, especially those held by African-American and Caribbean members. A congregation with African-American and European-American members in Chicago also attracts graduate students from several nations in Asia and Africa. An English-speaking congregation in Montreal gathers people of African descent from most of the

Caribbean nations, Canada, and the United States into negotiating their cultural differences and national loyalties both to build a faith community and to challenge governmental policies and public attitudes that perpetuate their linguistic and racial minority status in the city. The memberships of the nationally visible Glide Memorial Church in San Francisco and The Riverside Church in New York cut across race, ethnicity, social class, and sexual orientation.

This variation is evident in the three congregations central to this study. Cedar Grove United Methodist Church is located on the southern edge of Atlanta, Georgia. Its three hundred members include many European Americans who have been members of the church all their lives. Some are descendants of the families that established the congregation in 1828. Other members—African American, Sri Lankan, and Jamaican—joined the congregation during the past ten years. With a vibrant woman pastor, this congregation has sought to embody an alternative image of race relations in its community.

Oakhurst Presbyterian Church, in contrast, is located in one of the city's older suburban communities. Due to major demographic shifts in the city during the 1970s, the neighborhood quickly became predominantly black. The congregation decided to welcome these new neighbors. It called an African-American pastor. It continued to struggle—until the arrival of its present pastoral team nearly eight years prior to the beginning of this study—to maintain the privileged status of its European-American members. Following an intense power struggle initiated by the new pastor, a new vision of the congregation's mission emerged from an increasingly diverse constituency. Oakhurst now includes almost equal numbers of people with African and European ancestry, and a few people with Asian and Native American heritages. Among its members are doctors, lawyers, and university professors, as well as people with limited educational experience and economic resources.

The third congregation in our study is located in the center of one of the most culturally diverse neighborhoods in the southeastern United States. Major Korean, Chinese, Vietnamese, and Hispanic restaurants and shops line the nearby major streets. Within months after a new pastoral leadership team took up ministry in and through the congregation in 1990, the Administrative Council of Northwoods United Methodist Church voted to become a "multicultural church" and to reach out to these new neighbors. During our study the constituency of the congregation included people from twelve different nations. A Spanish-speaking ministry began during the year we were part of the congregation.

The experience of these congregations provides an alternative way to look at the changing religious scene among the voluntary mainline churches of the nation. Our attention will not be drawn to sweeping movements or trends but to the efforts of these three congregations to form a new kind of community of faith distinguished by the embrace of diversity and the celebration of differences. This decision limited the focus of the study to faith communities that emphasize the voluntary decision of their members to associate with one another. Culturally diverse Pentecostal and Roman Catholic churches provide intriguing insights into the dynamics of intercultural encounter. The negotiation of cultural perspectives and practices in these faith communities presumes, however, that significant sources for community loyalty are located in a common religious experience among Pentecostals, and in the authority of the church and its leaders among Roman Catholics.

STANDING OVER AGAINST TRADITION

E. Allen Richardson, in his study of the way people in the United States have responded to ethnic and religious pluralism, observes the nation has not been able to resolve a basic contradiction "deeply engrained in the nation's identity—the confrontation of two visions of American life characterized by diversity and homogeneity, pluralism and assimilation."[8] Richardson acknowledges, however, that the quest for assimilation and homogeneity and the metaphor of the nation as a melting pot have dominated the national imagination.

The interplay of diversity and unity, and homogeneity and heterogeneity in the traditions of forming communities of faith in the nation's history establish the context for the study of these three congregations. Two questions focused our research agenda on the interplay of congregational practices and understandings shaping the view of church members on what it means to be church and how that view of church informs its practices of nurturing its constituency: 1) Is there anything distinctive about a congregation that embraces cultural and racial diversity? 2) If so, how might these differences shape and inform the faith and identity of those who participate in its life and mission?

The task of raising these questions to consciousness made us sensitive to the depth of the witness of these congregations in standing over against the controlling traditions inherited from the past, which persist into the present, in part through the education of historically mainline churches. The church's education, in other words, helped 1) to maintain cultural and racial homogeneity in congregational life even as it sustained tolerance for theological and ecclesial diversity; and 2) to preserve, at the same time, the dominance of cultural traditions inherited from the nation's earliest settlers from northern Europe.[9]

The organization of the American Sunday School Union in 1824 by church leaders from prominent Protestant European-American denominations, for example, promoted a policy affirming denominational diversity in matters of belief and practice by refusing to publish anything that might be offensive to any denominational member. Robert Lynn and Elliot Wright have described the ambivalence to be found among denominational leaders of the Sunday school movement regarding missionary efforts among the African-American population.[10] Although important exceptions among both white and black church leaders should be noted, the relentless quest for financial support for mission Sunday schools on the frontier clearly limited the efforts of church leaders to extend their educational mission among blacks with equal aggressiveness.

Similar attitudes persist to this day in the careful orchestration of denominational elections to ensure racial, ethnic, and gender inclusivity while, at the same time, only appropriating perspectives and practices from the various members of the "representative body" that will not offend anyone else—especially the culturally dominant. The power of this preference for homogeneity and conformity in settings where people confront the racial and ethnic diversity of the nation means that the decision to embrace diversity in these three congregations has to be made over and over again.

The roots of the preference for a unity based on homogeneity and conformity run deep in the educational practices of mainline European-American churches.[11] For example, prior to the Civil War leaders of both Presbyterian and Methodist Churches in the South struggled to find ways to ensure the salvation of all people (including the slaves of church members) and maintain at the same time, the cultural values of a slaveholding society. Leaders in both churches produced catechisms recasting ancient formulas to ensure both a doctrine of universal salvation and the social and political differences that maintained, even advanced, the political advantage of the dominant race and culture. The perspective is evident in the opening lines of a catechism for slaves prepared by William Capers, a missionary to slaves and later a bishop of the Methodist Episcopal Church:

Minister.	My good children, tell me who made you?
Children.	God. He made all things.
Minister.	What did God make man out of?
Children.	The dust of the earth.
Minister.	What should this teach you?
Children.	*To be humble* [emphasis added].[12]

With a view of adult slaves as children and an emphasis on humility, obedience to authority becomes the dominant theme in the catechism. The religious instruction of slaves by the churches, in other words, perpetuated a status and power differential between the church's and the nation's blacks and whites.

From a quite different perspective European-American churches implemented governmental policies to remove Native American children by force from their homes in order to place them in distant boarding schools. Church and government officials hoped that in this isolation children and youth would forget their cultural traditions while they learned to farm and maintain homes in the ways of the dominant culture. Church education leaders sought explicitly to eliminate the potential for conflicts between dominant and dominated cultures by *subjugating* slaves and their cultural identity and *alienating* Native Americans from their cultural heritage. The rebellion of Nat Turner and the often bloody resistance of native tribes to the invasion from Europe fueled the fears that intensified this hegemonic quest of Americans of European descent.

The suppression of difference in church education policy and practice, however, did not only focus on race and culture. Throughout the nineteenth and early twentieth century, the growing sense of a national "manifest destiny" at work in the unfolding of the nation's identity and mission merged with the perception of the nation as a "melting pot" into which all non-Anglo-Saxon ethnic groups would blend. These two movements forged a sense of national destiny of leadership in the world. People shed their native cultural patterns and commitments in order to be remade in the Anglo-Saxon image established in the originating experiences of the nation's founders. New immigrant groups would contribute to the formation of a new cultural identity and national mission, but within the already established mold shaped by Anglo-Saxon social visions and values. Will Herberg's classic study of Protestants, Catholics, and Jews, published just prior to the Civil Rights Movement, articulates this viewpoint:

Despite widespread dislike of various aspects of British life, our relations cultural and spiritual, to our British heritage is vastly different and more intimate than is our relation to the cultural heritages of the later immigrant groups, who with their descendants compose a majority of the American people today. Our cultural assimilation has proceeded in essentially the same way as has our linguistic development—a few foreign words here and there, a few modifications of form, but still thoroughly and unquestionably English.[13]

It must be pointed out, however, that few efforts were made to consider how the cultures of people with black, brown, or yellow hues might meld into a new ethnic identity that took as its model the Anglo-Saxon. The point may be illustrated with a representative excerpt from a curriculum resource produced for children in the 1920s, at the height of one of the major waves of immigration in the United States:

> I know a little lad,
>   Perhaps you know him too.
> He wears the colors that we love,
>   The red and white and blue.
> His curly hair is red;
>   His skin is white to see,
> And the two big eyes of him
>   Are blue as blue can be.
> He is my little flag,
>   Dyed deeply, through and through
> With courage, truth and loyalty,—
>   The red and white and blue.[14]

As an ideal of the national character, the writer established clear boundaries for inclusion. The color symbolism clearly delineates who does and does not belong to the inner circle. Those whose eyes and hair coloring differed might experience prejudice and discrimination, but those who did not have skin as "white to see" would pose a problem to church leaders.[15] The ambivalence in educational resources for dominant-culture church children and youth toward African Americans, Asian Americans, Native Americans, and Hispanics or Latino/as continues into and beyond the 1960s. Since that pivotal decade the ambiguity of dominant-culture church folk toward the inclusion of all races and cultures has merged with a second perspective on ethnic and racial diversity to be found in the social policies of churches and governmental agencies.

This second perspective, as Richardson has pointed out, "sought unity in the midst of diversity." It did not assume that "consensus must be found in conformity" or in homogeneity. Its sources can also be traced back into the nineteenth century, when church advocates for a public school based their argument on the importance of a common opportunity for the children of all the (European) nations to learn together.[16] It becomes increasingly evident in resources for Sunday schools after the turn of the century. For example, in 1911, in a children's story paper, the text accompanying a drawing of children dressed to identify their country of origin as China, Japan, India, Holland, perhaps Italy and the United States (black and white) acknowledges such cultural differences as dress while emphasizing the love of God for all children, regardless of where they live or what their cultural identity might be.

> Our picture will help you think of some of the little people who are the flowers in the heavenly Father's world garden. Some are the little people of our own land. Some are little people who live in lands far away over the seas. The Gardener loves them all. He cares for them everyday.[17]

A vision of a world and nation consisting of people with distinctive cultural differences among church leaders did not occur in isolation. In an essay in *Nation* in 1915, Horace Kallen argued that the United States is "in the process of becoming a federal state not merely as a union of geographical and administrative unities, but also as a cooperation of cultural diversities, as a federation or commonwealth of national cultures." Alfredo Casteneda has recently observed that for Kallen the term "equal" as it "appeared in the Declaration of Independence, the Preamble, and amendments to the Constitution" may be equated with "difference."[18] As Richardson and others have pointed out, Kallen's vision of a mosaic rather than a melting pot for the nation eventually culminated during the 1960s in a vision of cultural pluralism for the nation and, among Christians, for its churches.

The influence of this perspective in the church's education again may be seen most clearly in the curriculum resources of dominant-culture denominations since the 1960s. Pictures in resources no longer displayed persons wearing a variety of culturally distinctive clothing. In their place, people from various racial backgrounds participated in shared activities in a common cultural environment. Pictures of classrooms depicted children and youth with different racial features. Illustrations of professional people encompassed both female and male, and black, yellow, and brown as well as white. In a parallel movement, black church presses began to require African-American images and stories to reflect the images and experiences of their constituencies.

A cursory survey of these changes in curricular resources might lead one to conclude that the vision of a melded national identity and global sense of responsibility was being realized. The terms of inclusion, however, had shifted rather than changed. The rhetoric in the church's educational resources drew on the images that Martin Luther King, Jr., and other civil-rights leaders set before the national consciousness. Pictures of black children sitting with white children translated his words into the images found in educational resources for church children. They presented a vision of what a congregation and its educational activities might look like. But little attention was given to the interplay of the cultural heritages among these racially and ethnically diverse groups. Instead, symbolic markers such as an Afro hairstyle in pictures or the use of the Japanese *haiku* poetic form in learning exercises contributed to the appearance of ethnic and racial diversity among church people.

It did not take long before the "newly included" in the rhetoric and educational resources of mainline denominations realized they might have a place in the new pluralism of church life but that the content of their heritage counted for little and their place depended on the repetition of a limited number of cultural symbols. A backlash occurred, first through the Black Power Movement, then through similar ethnic identity movements among Asians, Hispanics, and Native Americans. The publication of *Roots* by Alex Haley may have functioned as a symbolic watershed of opinion. From that point on, discussions on cultural diversity focused increasingly on issues of meaning and power in the differences diverse peoples bring to any common experience.

In the church the roots of this new perspective may have originated in the mission theology espoused by the World Council of Churches after World War II. One example may be seen in the study book Colin W. Williams wrote for the Third Assembly of the Council in New Delhi in 1961. Williams suggested that the "Church must 'let the world write the agenda' if it is to be truly the Servant of God's mission in today's alienated and fragmented society."[19] Williams transformed the hierarchical perspectives on the relationships of culturally diverse peoples in theological writings to the mutuality of all peoples located in their common origin in the love of God and their shared location on planet earth.

Certainly the conscientization of the power dynamics in any process of community socialization (including its formal patterns of education) precipitated by Paulo Freire's critique of traditional educational structures and processes enhanced the growing awareness among some pastors and church education leaders to the need for significantly different approaches to the processes of forming and sustaining congregational identity and to the theory and practices of religious education.[20] The fusion of Freire's pedagogical quest for an education to liberate people from economic and political oppression with the commitment of liberation theologians to empower communities of faith has influenced several prominent Christian education theorists, especially Letty Russell, Thomas Groome, Allen Moore, and Daniel Schipani.[21] Increasingly their influence is working its way into the educational practices of historically mainline denominations.

It is evident in curriculum resources, for example, in the growing tendency to locate the boundaries of human experience in the context of the world rather than the nation. Stories tend to emphasize the "insider" status of all peoples, not only within God's love, but in the fellowship of the human community. The names of people in stories and examples reflect the richness of the names by which people are called around the globe. Cultural differences are identified as facts of life rather than as artifacts to whet student curiosity. The influence of these educational perspectives has led a growing number of persons to call for a multi-ethnic or multicultural Christian education.[22] However, it has had little impact on denominational policies toward the nurture of faith perspectives at the congregational level. These perspectives do reveal, nonetheless, an increasingly appreciative national context for the efforts of those relatively isolated congregations across the country that have decided to stand over against deeply rooted and persistent cultural preference for cultural and racial homogeneity in congregational life by claiming the necessary contribution of ethnic and cultural diversity to the building up of Christian communities of faith.

METHOD OF STUDY

This study originated in the quest to understand something about the identity and educational mission of three quite different congregations with culturally diverse constituencies. We found few precedents to guide our efforts in either educational research or congregational studies. Most studies exploring the dynamics of racial or cultural interaction have focused on processes of integration, which by definition function within the framework of social and cultural assimilation. Most of the discussion on theological indigenization or multicultural education is theoretical or programmatic rather than empirical.[23] Although we assumed we would find many assimilationist assumptions and patterns at work in these congregations, we also believed that to begin with such a framework would blind us to the negotiations among the cultures in the formation of congregational identity and mission that countered the pervasive commitment to cultural assimilation in the nation.

Therefore, with little precedent to guide us, we proceeded to search for three congregations in the larger Atlanta metropolitan area. We looked for congregations with an established pastoral leadership, so our attention would not be diverted to the negotiations of a new pastor installed in a new congregation. Each church needed to have made a conscious commitment to cultural diversity for at least eight to ten years in order to provide some historical perspective on its experience.[24] We wanted a numerical balance among the various ethnic cultures gathered together in the congregation, assuming that equity in numbers might mean more horizontal than hierarchical political negotiations. We did ask judicatory leaders for suggestions of congregations that might meet these criteria. Most leads, however, came from persons we chanced to meet who had similar interests in culturally diverse communities of faith.

Two questions guided our study: 1) What view of church has been negotiated so far among the members of these congregations out of the interplay of their theological and cultural traditions? and 2) How does the congregation order its life to incorporate persons into the identity and mission of those ecclesial understandings? The first question directed our attention to congregational identity or its operational ecclesiology. The second led us to examine the educational patterns to be found in the life of the congregation.

Confronting Our Assumptions

Our quest to study intentionally diverse congregations began as a quest to understand their distinctiveness. Although we sought to employ an exploratory and open-ended stance, our reflections on our experience in these congregations illumined the assumptions we brought to the study. Four of these assumptions have significant methodological implications.

1) We did not approach these three congregations from a neutral or objective standpoint. Earlier work had already convinced us that the contemporary power dynamics among diverse cultures in nations like the United States, Canada, and Great Britain required the citizens of those societies to begin exploring ways to live in community by embracing rather than merely tolerating cultural pluralism. The intensification of ethnic, racial, and cultural conflict in the former Soviet Union and many of the nations of Africa, as well as struggles over "political correctness" and "white backlash" in the United States and Canada, only underscored for us the inadequacies of social and political strategies designed to control or assimilate those who differ from a dominant cultural group. We had been around enough culturally diverse congregations to wonder if their embrace of diversity might not embody a new form of community distinguished by their affirmation of diversity. Were these congregations living on the edge of our future? That question was enough to prompt our curiosity about what distinguished them from the majority of congregations, which experiences cultural difference as a stumbling block to the nurture of a common ecclesial identity.

2) We approached this study persuaded that as we approach the end of the millennium we are living into an emerging paradigm shift radically re-ordering our sense of the nature of reality. Variously called by scholars a *postmodern, post-enlightenment,* or *post-positivist* era, it is characterized by an increasing awareness of the limits (among other things) of the patterns of objectivity and rationality inherited from the Enlightenment, which have guided most studies of human experience for at least the past two hundred years.[25]

The implications of this emerging paradigm for the researcher are significant. In an essay on organizational research David L. Clark identifies several differences between traditional and post-positivist research. These include attention to complexity rather than simplicity in the quest to understand the nature of things; holographic rather than mechanical metaphors in social and organizational analysis; and mutual rather than linear causality as a means to understanding the nature of change. Perhaps most significant for the initial stages of research design is the assumption that the stance of the researcher is perspectival rather than objective.[26] In this new paradigm pluralism is not a problem to be addressed, but a descriptor of the reality of the researcher's context.

3) Perhaps the most troublesome dynamic in our study emerged from our growing awareness of the influence of the research team's own ethnic identities and cultural experiences on ways we collected data as well as on our interpretations of what we saw and heard. One European-American research team member, for example, discovered after several weeks that he had only set up interviews with white church members because they immediately suggested a time to meet while black members expressed their willingness to talk with a "give me a call sometime." Subconsciously, at least, he misinterpreted this indirect response to be a kind of reluctance or resistance. In another instance, an African-American member of the team had difficulty identifying the dynamics of the worship life at Oakhurst because she did not find the liturgical praise patterns she associated with vital worship. Our field notes and discussions increasingly revealed that we viewed the same patterns of association and interaction and the meanings attributed to time and space in the life and work of these congregations in a variety of ways.[27] When we would seek to identify sources to these differences, many would be located in the variations of our cultural perspectives. Our research, in other words, made us increasingly conscious of the influence of our own ethnic identities on our perceptions of what we heard and saw as researchers.

4) Some would call these congregations *multicultural*. A review of the literature, however, made us cautious about the way our use of this term might influence what we observed and heard. Although the word *multicultural* was apparently coined in a 1941 book review to describe a way of life that stood over against "nationalism, national prejudice and behavior,"[28] it has only come into vogue since the 1970s. Some use the term to designate the demographic diversity of the nation.[29] More typical, however, are the variety of ideologies people seem to associate with the term—ranging from assimilation into the dominant culture to advocacy for the social reconstruction of society.[30] The range of meanings associated with the term and the diversity of feelings it evokes among different groups of people limited its usefulness as a research category in this study.

Making Sense of the Data

James Hopewell observed that "a group of people cannot regularly gather for what they feel to be religious purposes without developing a complex network of signals and symbols and conventions—in short, a subculture—that gains its own logic and then functions in a way peculiar to that group." This discovery pushed his research beyond the obvious elements in the lives of religious communities and institutions—creeds, structures of governance, and programs—to the "symbols and signals of the world" gathered and grounded into "the congregation's own idiom." This insight distinctively shaped congregational studies in general and established the framework for our research. We followed his advice that "the fullest and most satisfying way to study the culture of a congregation is to live within its fellowship and learn directly how it interprets its experience and generates its behavior."[31] We approached these congregations as participant observers seeking to develop a thick description from our encounters with the stories, symbols, and signs distinguishing their sense of identity and mission.[32]

We discovered that the narrative structure of a congregation contains several levels. At this point Elliott Eisner's distinctions among explicit, implicit, and null curriculum helped us describe the kinds of narratives we heard and told each other. Some stories were *explicit*, freely and frequently shared, and widely affirmed. They included narratives from biblical and church tradition. Others told about local people, events, and circumstances. They were granted authority by being repeated from the pulpit and by teachers and congregational leaders in class sessions and administrative meetings. Their repetition in public forums sanctioned them as official descriptions of congregational values and practices.

Other stories lay beneath the surface of the official and public narratives. Rarely shared, they surfaced when we would ask "why" and "how come" questions in relation to some sign, symbol, or story lacking obvious explanation. These *implicit* stories made evident assumed relationships and structures in the congregation and between the congregation and community. They often challenged assumptions we made initially about the congregations based on the stories integral to their public discourse. They became significant clues to untangling complex and persistent themes in the narratives of congregational identity. They pushed us, for example, to look beyond the traditional male-gender language patterns in the narratives of Cedar Grove to the highly charged feminist narratives embodied in the leadership patterns revolving around the interactions of the members of the congregation and their female pastor.

Then we discovered in each congregation gaps in their narratives. Stories of some events and relationships had been repressed. Some had been forgotten. Others simply did not exist. Some we did not understand. The presence of these "stories" became obvious in the quiet spaces that would follow our questions, in the gaps in congregational communication, in the resistance to tracing the origins of a sign or symbol in congregational life, and in their sudden irruption when some situation or event would not be contained within a description of the operating framework of the congregation. These unspoken stories, making up what Eisner has called the *null* curriculum, seemed to cluster typically around dynamics of racism, classism, and sexism.[33]

When we reflected on these stories we discovered that they seemed to revolve around certain contextually paradigmatic narratives which gathered up and evoked certain signifying words, images, or actions. We had rediscovered through our own work insights deeply rooted in Hopewell's study of congregational life. A congregation communicates its identity and mission primarily through narrative. Stories seem to be the only vehicle comprehensive enough to convey the rich complexity of congregational life and to make evident the connections among events, values, and beliefs. Stories create plausibility out of seemingly unrelated events and circumstances, and they provide images, structures, or models that give meaning and purpose to the way a congregation perceives itself in the world that surrounds it.[34]

The stories also tended to cluster around certain signs or symbols integral to the congregation's vocabulary for its identity and mission. Again, Hopewell's insight that the narratives of a congregation form patterns of meaning "so regular" they signify a group's perceived and expressed identity, pointed to the potential meanings of the stories we had been collecting.[35] The signs established an order to the narratives we heard and were telling each other. Some were visual, for example, the brown face and arms of Jesus in an Oakhurst stained-glass window, the dual entrances into Cedar Grove's sanctuary and gym, Northwoods' worship space ordered around a central communion table. Other signs were verbal, for example, "we are family" at Cedar Grove, or the repetition of the image of Christ breaking down "the dividing wall . . . between us" (Eph 2:14) in the life of Oakhurst, or St. John's vision of the "multitudes from every nation, from all tribes, and peoples and languages, standing before the throne and the Lamb" (Rv 7:9), heard repeatedly at Northwoods. Other signs were active, such as, the pastor walking a newly baptized child down the central aisle at Oakhurst, or the pastor using the whole space of the sanctuary as the platform for his leadership of worship at Northwoods.

We began by first *identifying and naming signs* that established an interpretive trajectory for stories we heard, saw, and told. We did not begin the project recognizing this task as the first in the interpretive process. It became apparent to us as the repeated exercise of reviewing our field notes and rehearsing the stories indicated patterns of relationships among them. In the act of naming signs, however, we became increasingly aware that our choices reflected meanings on the part of church members and the research team based on what Eisner has called "antecedent knowledge."[36] Meanings drawn from our prior religious experience and academic studies influenced our perceptions of the potentialities in the sign of Jesus holding the hands of black and white children in the stained-glass window of Cedar Grove, for example. Foster had previously explored ways in which the relationship of Jesus to children has been seen by artists through history and around the world and by the writers and editors of church school curriculum resources in the United States. Other team members brought to the naming of that same sign personal experiences of interracial relationships and understandings of racial politics from our academic studies.

A second step in making sense of the stories engaged us in the effort to *weave the stories* that cluster around each sign into a larger story or "meta-story" integral to the identity and vocation of the congregation.[37] We discovered several recurring thematic patterns in the aggregate of stories. Again Eisner's categories of explicit, implicit, and null curriculum proved to be helpful. In the interpretive process at least three kinds of narratives made up the *explicit* themes: 1) stories of our encounters as researchers with the sign; 2) stories explicating the history of the sign; and 3) stories conveying the shared meanings of the sign for members of the congregation.

We had to listen and watch for the *implicit* themes. The repetition of explicit themes sometimes brought them to our attention. One such implicit theme centered around the meaning and place of children in the church. For example, the children and youth of Cedar Grove are very visible. They are present for most congregational activities. Their voices are heard in congregational gatherings. Several asked us questions during the meetings we held in the congregation. Ten of the more than thirty respondents to a prayer request by the pastor one Sunday morning during worship were children. People of the congregation work in a variety of places as advocates for children. Stories of their involvement in the church's after-school program, summer day camp, or in the P.T.A. of the local school filled our research notes. The explicit theme of celebrating and advocating for children was quite evident. But not all the stories we heard celebrated the presence of children and youth. Some revealed frustration among European-American adults about "lack of commitment" to the schedule of Sunday school and other children's activities among African-American children. Other stories indicated ambiguity in the congregation about ways to be more responsive to the clearly minority number of European-American children in its midst. An implicit theme of conflicting cultural assumptions, in other words, about the purposes and schedules of Sunday school helped to fill out the stories integral to the sign of Jesus and the children.

A third layer of themes (corresponding to Eisner's *null* curriculum) contributing to the weaving of the narratives around the various signs had to do with the silences in congregational stories and with the stories that had been repressed or shoved to the margins of corporate consciousness. For example, in a congregation consisting primarily of younger African-American families and middle-aged and older European-American families, congregational attention simply did not have to focus upon the daily interactions of black and white children and youth, issues of sexuality related to cross-cultural dating, or contrasting cultural expectations in child-rearing practices.

The third step we employed in the interpretive process of congregational stories centered on *identifying and exploring the significance of the sign.* Several implications from our research efforts illuminate this step. When the research effort begins in a partnership of researcher and congregation, the interpretive activity must include both parties. This means, as Charles Gerkin has reminded us, that our efforts grow out of the "merger or fusion" of horizons of meaning and understanding that we each bring to the interpretive moment. The activity is inherently dialogical.[38]

In pluralistic contexts like these three congregations, the interpretive process is dynamic and fluid. The dialogical character of the interpretive event encompasses more than a common horizon of understanding on the part of the congregation and the researcher (although that may exist). It also includes the possibility for a variety of horizons of understanding to be found in the diversity of experiences present in the congregation's constituency. Interpretations consequently are local, situational, and multiple. They are evocative and directional rather than definitive and generalizable. They contribute to the narrative life of the congregation by refining, elaborating, or assessing the adequacy of prior understandings of the signs integral to congregational identity and vocation. They do not function as objective principles for congregational action.

The dialogical character of the interpretive act requires that the researcher take the context of interpretation as seriously as the processes for observation and listening. The partners to the interpretive act in the congregation are the members themselves. Indeed we often found ourselves facilitating the conversation among pastors and church members about their understandings of the meanings evoked by the larger narratives the researchers helped to bring to awareness.

The roles shifted when we began to interpret the narratives of these congregations for the church-at-large and the academy. At this point the congregation became consultant to our interpretive efforts. We had, without recognizing its larger implications, built this step into the process from the beginning, when we told the governing bodies of the congregations that representatives from the churches would be asked to review materials we prepared for publication.

SUMMARY

Some congregations across the nation seek to embody the visions of racial, cultural, and class heterogeneity rooted in biblical visions of the kingdom of God and the dreams of the Civil Rights Movement. They challenge assumptions of homogeneity integral to voluntary notions of congregational identity and explore alternative patterns of relating across the boundaries of race, ethnicity, and/or class that inform the power dynamics of the church's and the nation's diverse population. These challenges do not come easily. Hegemonic patterns exist, for the most part, subconsciously in our corporate memories. In the embrace of difference, the pain of those patterns rises to the surface and must be addressed constructively if the community is to be vital to its members.

These emerging forms of voluntary communities of diversity also shaped our research agenda and methods in the three congregations we studied. Through these congregations we discovered some of our own cultural biases. We learned quickly that normative descriptions from prior congregational studies diminished our capacity to discern distinctive patterns and relationships in their common lives. The interpretive framework for examining the data from our study emerged from our conversations with one another and the leadership of each congregation. That framework establishes the structure for the rest of the book. We turn now to stories of Cedar Grove, Oakhurst, and Northwoods churches, with attention to the *signs* we identified that give distinctive content to their identities as communities of faith.

Notes

1. Wade Clark Roof and William McKinney, *American Mainline Religion: Its Changing Shape and Future* (New Brunswick: Rutgers University Press, 1987), 3.

2. An illustrative sample of the literature exploring the changing demography and character of American U.S. literature includes Dean M. Kelly, *Why Conservative Churches Are Growing: A Study in the Sociology of Religion* (New York: Harper and Row, 1972); Tex Sample, *U.S. Lifestyles and Mainline Churches: A Key to Reaching People in the 90's* (Louisville: Westminster/John Knox Press, 1990); Virgilio Elizondo, *Galilean Journey: The Mexican American Promise* (Maryknoll, NY: Orbis Books, 1983); William R. Hutchison, *Between the Times: The Travail of Protestant Establishment in America 1900-1960* (Cambridge: Cambridge University Press, 1989); Martin E. Marty, *The Public Church: Mainline, Evangelical, Catholic* (New York: Crossroad Publishing Company, 1981); Nancy Tatom Ammerman, *Baptist Battles: Social Change and Religious Conflict in the Southern Baptist Convention* (New Brunswick: Rutgers University Press, 1990).

3. Robert N. Bellah, Richard Madsen, William M. Sullivan, Ann Swidler, Steven M. Tipton, *Habits of the Heart: Individualism and Commitment in American Life* (Berkeley: University of California Press, 1985), viii; Robert Wuthnow, *The Struggle for America's Soul: Evangelicals, Liberals, and Secularism* (Grand Rapids: William P. Eerdman's Publishing Co., 1989), vi-viii; Roof and McKinney, 3-5, 40.

4. In using the phrase *historically mainline,* we refer to that group of denominations that have historically functioned as the "dominant, culturally established faiths held by the majority of Americans." Roof and McKinney argue that the contemporary dynamics of pluralism have effectively expanded the use of the term *mainline* to include many groups across both religious and racial boundaries (Roof and McKinney, 6).

5. E. Allen Richardson, *Strangers in This Land: Pluralism and the Response to Diversity in the United States* (New York: The Pilgrim Press, 1988), 127.

6. The task of identifying congregations that encompass significant racial and cultural diversity did not prove to be easy. To begin, no consensus exists around the categories that might distinguish difference based on race or culture. The U.S. Census Bureau, for example, mixes racial categories (white, black) with cultural categories (Native American, Asian). Despite this confusion some judicatories have begun to request membership statistics that include some kind of breakdown on race and/or culture. In some cases, these statistics only reveal the extent to which a congregation shifts membership from one cultural or racial group to another as its follows the demographic changes of its neighborhood. Such congregations tend to be labelled "transitional churches." This identification tends to underscore the tendency among judicatory leaders to identify congregations not by the

character of their diversity but by qualifiers of homogeneity. For example, in two of the churches we studied, some denominational leaders described the congregations as black (because they once were white and now are at least 50 percent black, despite congregational self-identification as being *both black and white*. Consequently, we began to identify congregations primarily by following up on leads from people who knew or had heard about congregations that valued racial and cultural diversity as an integral component in their identity as communities of faith.

7. Sharon Welch describes the impetus to reciprocity of mutual critique in a communicative ethic that values the interplay of pluralism and social responsibility. Such an ethic "takes as its standpoint the interaction between 'concrete others.'" It shifts the power dynamics between groups from hierarchical to horizontal patterns ("An Ethic of Solidarity and Difference," in *Postmodernism, Feminism, and Cultural Politics: Redrawing Educational Boundaries*, ed. Henry A. Giroux [Albany: State University of New York Press, 1991], 88-89).

8. Richardson, 21.

9. In *The Transit of Civilization*, Edward Eggleston, a prominent turn-of-the-century historian, described the power of tradition to persist over time, challenging in the process, the popular notion that the United States was a distinctively new society. Eggleston traces major themes and practices in the national character back to their English roots (*The Transit of Civilization: From England to America in the Seventeenth Century* [Boston: Beacon Press, 1959 {1900}]). He significantly influenced a similarly revisionist approach to the educational history of the nation in the work of Bernard Bailyn (*Education in the Forming of American Society: Needs and Opportunities for Study* [New York: Vintage Books, 1960]), Lawrence A. Cremin (*Traditions of American Education* [New York: Basic Books, Inc., Publishers, 1977]); and Robert W. Lynn and Elliot Wright (*The Big Little School: Two Hundred Years of the Sunday School* [Birmingham: Religious Education Press, 1980]).

10. Lynn and Wright, 61-65.

11. For a more extensive discussion of the educational practices of dominant culture churches among minority populations in the United States, see Charles R. Foster, "Double Messages: Ethnocentrism in the Education of the Church," *Religious Education* 82 (Summer 1987): 447-68; and "Imperialism in the Education of the Church," in *Religious Education* 86 (Winter 1991): 145-55.

12. William Capers, *Catechism for Little Children: The Missions . . . of South Carolina* (Charleston: J.S. Burges, 1833), 3.

13. Will Herberg, *Protestant, Catholic, Jew: An Essay in American Religious Sociology* (Garden City: Doubleday, 1955), 34.

14. Abbie Farwell Brown, "The Little Flag," *Picture Story Paper* (Methodist Episcopal Church) 54 (June 10, 1923), 2. We discovered a clue to the persistence of this racial image through the centuries in Simon Schama's exploration of the relationship of landscape and memory in Western social

and political life and thought, in which he notes that for Tacitus, the Roman historian, Germanic peoples seemed to be the "true indigens, sprung from the black earth of their native land." Tacitus associated himself with "the opinions of those who hold that in the peoples of Germany there has been given to the world a race unmixed by intermarriage with other races, a peculiar people and pure, like no-one but themselves, whence it comes that their physique, so far as can be said with their vast numbers is identical: fierce blue eyes, red hair, tall frames, powerful" (quoted in Simon Schama, *Landscape and Memory* [New York: Alfred A. Knopf, 1995], 82).

15. Anya Royce Peterson observes that this process of establishing boundaries of ethnic identity involves two actions. In the first, symbolic markers like the colors emphasized in the poem establish boundaries from within a group to distinguish it from other groups. At the same time, those excluded may reinforce those distinctions in ways that contribute to ethnic stereotyping on the part of the first group. Her point illuminates the difficulty groups have when they seek to dismiss the effects of such markers after decades, even centuries of use (*Ethnic Identity: Strategies of Diversity* [Bloomington: Indiana University Press, 1982], 29).

16. Richardson, 26-27. For an example of the rhetoric of the free public school advocates of the mid-nineteenth century, see Horace Bushnell, "Common Schools," in *Building Eras in Religion* (New York: Charles Scribner's Sons, 1881), 76, 97. The issue for Bushnell was not so much national or ethnic diversity as the differences between immigrant Catholic and "American" Protestant. He promoted the common school as the best place to build mutual understanding across these differences in the education of citizens.

17. *Picture Story Paper* 42 (October 18, 1911): Part 2.

18. Quoted by Alfredo Casteneda, "Persisting Ideological Issues of Assimilation in America," in *Cultural Pluralism*, ed. Edgar G. Epps (Chicago: University of Chicago Press, 1974), 61.

19. Colin W. Williams, *Where in the World? Changing Forms of the Church's Witness* (New York: National Council of the Churches of Christ in the U.S.A., 1963), 75.

20. See Paulo Freire, *Pedagogy of the Oppressed* (New York: Continuum Publishing Company, 1986), chaps. 1-2.

21. See Thomas H. Groome, *Christian Religious Education: Sharing Our Story and Vision* (San Francisco: Harper & Row Publishers, 1980) and *Sharing Faith: A Comprehensive Approach to Religious Education and Pastoral Ministry* (HarperSanFrancisco, 1991); Letty M. Russell, *The Future of Partnership* (Philadelphia: The Westminster Press, 1979) and *Growth in Partnership* (Philadelphia: The Westminster Press, 1981); Allen J. Moore, "A Social Theory of Religious Education," in *Religious Education as Social Transformation*, ed. Allen J. Moore (Birmingham: Religious Education Press, 1989); Daniel J. Schipani, *Religious Education Encounters Liberation Theology* (Birmingham: Religious Education Press, 1988).

22. Most of the calls for a more explicit embrace of cultural diversity in the education of the church are to be found in articles written for a lay

readership in the local church. One of the most thorough discussions may be found in *Religious Education* 87 (Spring 1992), 170-217.

23. Christine E. Sleeter and Carl A. Grant, "An Analysis of Multicultural Education in the United States," *Harvard Educational Review* 57 (November 1987), 433-34.

The literature on contextualization and inculturation expanded significantly during the 1980s. Robert Schreiter's *Constructing Local Theologies* (Maryknoll, NY: Orbis Books, 1986) has been especially helpful in identifying patterns of theological reflection in the congregations of this study.

Important examples of research into *multicultural* education do exist. William R. Myers contrasts the cultural influences in an ethnographic study of the youth ministries of two congregations: *Black and White Styles of Youth Ministry: Two Congregations in America* (New York: The Pilgrim Press, 1991). Alan Peshkin explores "the play of ethnicity" in his ethnographic study of a California high school and community: *The Color of Strangers, The Color of Friends: The Play of Ethnicity in School and Community* (Chicago: The University of Chicago Press, 1991). In a series of monographs culminating in *Family Ministry Through Cross-Cultural Education: A Final Report*, Taylor and June McConnell describe their efforts to cross the communication barriers of three cultures in New Mexico (Evanston: The Leiffer Bureau of Social and Religious Research [Garrett-Evangelical Theological Seminary], 1990). I have also had extended conversations with Mary Elizabeth Moore of the School of Theology at Claremont regarding her own approach to cross-cultural research methodologies in her yet unpublished study of several ethnic congregations.

24. When a congregation meeting these criteria withdrew from the research project, we decided to work with a congregation that had made the decision to work toward becoming multicultural only two years before. This congregation's struggles with the consequences of that decision actually helped to illumine more distant first steps in the other two congregations.

25. This literature is vast and growing. A range of examples pertinent to our work include Robert Bellah, et. al., *Habits of the Heart*; Richard Rorty, *Objectivity, Relativism, and Truth*; Letty Russell, *The Future of Partnership* and *Growth in Partnership*; Stanley Aronowitz and Henry A. Giroux, *Postmodern Education: Politics, Culture, and Social Criticism* (Minneapolis: The University of Minnesota Press, 1991); Rebecca S. Chopp, *The Power to Speak: Feminism, Language, God* (New York: The Crossroad Publishing Company, 1991).

26. David L. Clark, "Emerging Paradigms in Organizational Theory and Research," in *Organizational Theory and Inquiry: The Paradigm Revolution*, ed. Yvonna S. Lincoln (Beverly Hills: Sage Publications, 1985), 69ff.

27. These terms, identified by Edward T. Hall as primary message systems, are found in the study of any culture. Other terms highlight the dynamics of subsistence, sexuality, learning, play, defense, and exploitation of resources. These terms make up what Hall calls "the vocabulary of culture" (*The Silent Language*, 45-60).

28. See William Safire, "Multi Multi-," *The New York Times Magazine* (February 23, 1992), 20.

29. For example, Martha Farnsworth Riche observes that contemporary immigration and birthrate trends "signal a transition to a multicultural society" in the United States. If these trends continue the nation will have "no racial or ethnic majority during the 21st century" ("We're All Minorities Now," in *American Demographics* [October 1991], 26-29).

30. This point has been made in a review of the literature on multicultural education by Sleeter and Grant. They describe how educators and researchers use the term *multicultural* to 1) espouse the value of cultural diversity; 2) promote patterns of interaction that respect human rights and cultural diversity among diverse peoples; 3) advocate alternative life choices for people; 4) affirm the necessity of equal opportunity and justice for all peoples; and 5) promote the equitable distribution of power among diverse ethnic/cultural communities as well as create and maintain social, political, and economic relationships to enhance all peoples (Sleeter and Grant, 421-44).

31. Hopewell, 5, 88.

32. Clifford Geertz, following the work of Gilbert Ryle, identifies the task of creating thick description, as "an elaborate venture in" the "piled-up structures of inference and implication" to be found in any signifying act or event of human interaction (Geertz, 7-10).

33. Elliott Eisner, *The Educational Imagination* (New York: Macmillan Publishing Company, 1979), chap. 5; Maria Harris, *Teaching and Religious Imagination* (New York: Harper & Row, 1987), 100ff.

34. Hopewell, 46-47.

35. Ibid., 48-49.

36. Eisner, 64-67.

37. In this sense we developed one approach to articulating what Robert J. Schreiter has called a local theology—those theological assumptions that inform the commitments and actions of particular communities (see Robert J. Schreiter, *Constructing Local Theologies* [Maryknoll, NY: Orbis Books, 1985], 1-21).

38. Charles V. Gerkin, *The Living Human Document: Re-Visioning Pastoral Counseling in a Hermeneutical Mode* (Nashville: Abingdon Press, 1984), 44-45.

2

CEDAR GROVE
UNITED METHODIST CHURCH

INTRODUCTION

Weekly worship establishes a rhythmic counterpoint to the episodic events that shape the life of Cedar Grove Church. Our introduction to this interplay of continuity and surprise occurred during our first visit as a research team to the congregation. The September morning was already warm when we pulled into the large parking lot built, we later discovered, after a tornado had blown down a host of pine trees surrounding the church. To our left a large predominantly steel building overwhelmed the smaller brick building housing the sanctuary and several Sunday school rooms. One of the ushers and a young girl greeted us at the door. We were early. As members of the church whom we had already met arrived they came over to our seats to greet us. The small room, seating perhaps 150 people, looked as if it recently had been redecorated. White walls and chancel furniture created an almost pristine feeling. The low ceiling and close proximity of pulpit and pew contributed to the sense of intimacy. Our attention was drawn to the rather contemporary lines of the figures in the stained-glass windows behind the choir loft and on the right wall. My attention was immediately caught by the image of Jesus holding the hands of dark-skinned and light-skinned children.

This was the first Sunday in September. Like most United Methodist congregations, this meant communion would be celebrated. The robed choir entered the sanctuary from a side door. Rev. Martha, as all members referred to their pastor, slipped into her chair behind

the pulpit after them. After the prelude, she greeted the congregation: "Welcome to Cedar Grove United Methodist Church. We are
family here. We want you to feel at home in this place." "Home" did
seem an appropriate way to talk about our initial feelings of the
place. Prior to the prelude people greeted and talked to each other.
Rev. Martha was not wearing a robe. She spoke in a conversational
tone—more like the hostess at a dinner party of close friends giving
instructions and guiding the conversation among everyone present.
Following a few announcements, including a general introduction
of the research team to the congregation, we joined in singing the
first hymn and then began to follow the order of worship for communion found in the hymnal.

Prior to the service of worship Rev. Martha asked me to assist in
the distribution of communion elements. When that time came in
the service I joined her at the communion table. She moved from
person to person kneeling at the communion rail giving each a piece
of bread. A moment or two later I gave each person a small glass of
grape juice. As we came to a tall, athletic-looking, young African-
American man, she leaned over to give him the bread, looked him
squarely in the eye and said, "This represents the body of Christ and
that means you and I are brother and sister." Without a break in her
pace she moved on to the next person.

A look out over the congregation would certainly challenge common assumptions about who makes up a typical family in the southeastern United States. Its designated leader was a woman with a
cultural and racial heritage originating in Europe. Slightly more than
half of the adults and most of the children were black. Most but not
all of the rest were white. One family consisted of a black father, a
white mother and two sons. A woman, whom we later discovered
was from Sri Lanka, sat in a pew with several older white women.
The choir included almost equal numbers of black and white members. When the ushers came forward to receive the offering one was
black and the other white. As I pondered Rev. Martha's description
of this congregation as a family my attention refocused on the stained-
glass window depicting Jesus with dark-skinned and light-skinned
children. Although we had come expecting to discover how a congregation that had been described to us as striving to be an *integrated* church in the deep south understood itself, we had not expected
its members to describe themselves in familial terms. To be family
here obviously meant something quite distinctive.

Almost each week brought another account of a researcher being
surprised by another event or story. An example occurred during a

consultation our research team sponsored for pastors of congregations experiencing increasing cultural diversity. The pastors of the three churches in our study were present. During the course of one session Rev. Martha began to recount the story of a critical moment fairly early in the struggle over the dynamics of race in the future of Cedar Grove's ministry:

> A *big man in the church* [emphasis hers] called me up to tell me that if I took in another black member, he was leaving the church and he would take everything he had given the church with him. If he left that meant he would take about thirty-five others—mostly relatives with him.
>
> The next Sunday morning I took in another black family anyway. They are now among the strongest leaders in the church. I talked to some trustees about changing locks on the church doors, which they did that afternoon. We knew he would make good on his threat, so that night a bunch of us were waiting in the bushes to see what he would do when he came to the church to get his stuff. He came all right. He tried his key first in the front door, then went around to the side doors. He looked so frustrated! And all the time we were out there in the bushes just laughing to beat heck.

Of course, out in the bushes were European Americans who had shared much with that man and his family over many years in the life of that church. To be "in the bushes" meant, for them, deciding against the racism deeply rooted in the church and community and against long-time friends and church colleagues who could not bring themselves to acknowledge racism's threat to the life of the church and community.

A third episode illuminating something of the character of Cedar Grove Church occurred near the end of our year of study. Although the church owned a sizeable piece of land, the building had been constructed next to the back property line. Owners of this piece of property informed the church that they planned to put it on the market. The church did not have discretionary funds to buy it, but the notice prompted much talk on the front lawn after worship, while the men mowed the lawn on Saturdays, over the phone, and around the dinner table. Young people not only overheard these conversations but as the weeks went by, began to express their opinions. It quickly became apparent they felt strongly about the necessity of buying that piece of property. A church conference was called. A good crowd showed up including more than thirty-five children and youth who expected to have a say and a vote on the matter. Apparently church leaders assumed they would as well. Although their vote would not stand up in court, children and youth participated in the secret ballot to stretch the financial resources of the congregation to buy the land. We never heard of any program sponsored by Cedar Grove Church to discuss the role of children and youth in church; they just seemed to assume children and youth had a voice in church affairs.

One must probe the history of the congregation for sources to the two most pressing issues affecting the quality and character of its ministry in the larger community—family generational fragmentation and racism. In a fashion similar to many other rural congregations, Cedar Grove has existed, for the most part, as a *family* church. Organized by ancestors of some current members in 1828, it was originally called Morris Chapel after the most prominent of those families. Suspicion of hierarchical and external authority among the leading families led the congregation to participate in the creation of the lay-centered Methodist Protestant Church prior to the Civil War. As the only congregation in the community until after World War II, it functioned as the religious family for all the members of the community, including Methodists, Presbyterians, Baptists, and others. This congregational family originally included the slaves of members, who, following the social customs of the day, sat in the back pews. Their denigrated social and political status was reinforced for eternity with burial in a separate section of the church cemetery. Apparently these "members" left the church during Reconstruction.

Cedar Grove shared the patriarchal and racially homogenous images of church typical of the region through World War II. At that point its Baptist members withdrew to form their own congregation. The city, with increasing momentum, encroached upon the dairy farms surrounding the church, radically altering the rhythms and relationships that governed its life. With the construction of a new international airport, the church found itself under the landing approach of aircraft. The county began paving roads. City water, gas, and electrical lines hastened the loss of the traditional rural character of the community. Members gradually gave up their dairy farms to find work in county government and nearby industries. During the mid-1970s people (mostly European American) moving to the city to take advantage of the rapidly growing economy settled in new subdivisions springing up around the church. They intruded upon decades-old patterns of family interrelationships in the community. Even larger numbers of African Americans fled into the Cedar Grove community from the destruction of their neighborhoods in the city to accommodate the interstate highway system and a new sports arena. The relational dynamics sustaining the values and perspectives of church and community members increasingly fragmented.

Within a short time congregational expectations shifted from growth to the fear of dying. Young European-American families, including those who had grown up in the church and community, fled the growing immigration of African Americans into the neighborhood and schools. The Cedar Grove Church family lost its children. Church leaders became concerned about its future. With the encouragement of their pastor, members voted to welcome anyone who came to church. But this did not prevent the gradual decline in membership and morale. When the bishop moved their pastor to a new appointment, five men rejected the "opportunity to fill this congregation's pulpit" before Rev. Martha was offered and accepted the challenge of serving the congregation. She moved into the parsonage in January 1981. Her husband and teen-age children soon followed.

Rev. Martha presided over the final years of membership decline from more than 300 in the mid-1970s to a low of 243 in 1989. In 1992 congregational membership stood at 291—a significant jump. Of this number approximately 60 percent are African American and 40 percent European American. The younger members (under 45) and children are predominantly African American. Most European Americans are of middle age or older with some of their college-age or still single young adult children also attending. Other members have Sri Lankan and Jamaican heritages. Most congregants own homes within a few miles of the church and identify themselves as middle class. Teachers, middle managers, small business owners, and civil servants have replaced the long heritage of people whose occupations connected them closely to the soil. Although most new members are of African-American heritage, the congregation continues to attract some European Americans into its fold. Demographic patterns in the area make the recruitment of significant numbers of new members of European descent however, increasingly difficult.

As a family church, Cedar Grove's character has been radically changed. It no longer relies on kinship or length of historical relationship. Patriarchal and European-American cultural hegemony has been shattered. A new image has begun to fill the imaginations of church folk—one that celebrates interdependent equity among black and white members and which involves the mutuality of black and white responsibility in shaping the future for the children of the church and community.

COMMUNITY OF TEACHING AND LEARNING

Traditional educational structures certainly do not account for the vitality and energy of this congregation. One researcher found this out on her first Sunday. She arrived early to observe one of the Sunday school classes for children. She found her way into a room where she saw some children. After a while it became obvious that the teacher would not be coming or would be very late. Someone poked her head in the door and asked the researcher if she minded teaching. "Of course not," she replied.

Several of the European-American women who had given leadership to the Sunday school twenty and thirty years before simply shake their heads over younger members of the church who have not taken the Sunday school as seriously as they had in the past. Teachers and students arrive late. Teachers do not attend denominationally sponsored training sessions. Despite her popularity as pastor, Rev. Martha's attempt to start and teach a young adult class only attracted an average attendance of five to six persons.

The dynamics of teaching and learning at Cedar Grove do not occur so much in classrooms as in the conversations of people in the congregation and community. This is not an unstructured process, although it took us most of the year we spent in the congregation to begin to discern its elements.[1] We experienced it, even though we did not recognize the pattern at the time, in an intensified form within our first month. As we found a seat for worship on this particular Sunday morning, we noted that three rows of pews had been marked off with a rope. Within a few minutes several strapping young men took their place in one of the pews. Gradually others filled the pews and several more sat among the congregation. Everyone seemed to know what was going on but us (an oft-repeated experience over the year, because we were not always in the conversation loop). Finally someone leaned over to tell us they were members of the local high school football team.

We knew church members followed the progress of the football team closely. Several youth in the church were members of the team. Others served as cheerleaders. Rev. Martha jogged on the football field daily and talked with the coaches and youth. She joined one of the African-American men in recruiting Cedar Grove Church members for a cheering section for home and away games. When the football team arrived on this Sunday morning, conversation, in other words, had already begun. When Rev. Martha greeted the congregation with her frequent refrain, "Welcome to Cedar Grove Church, we are family here," we slowly began to realize that she and many others in the church perceived the members of this football team to be part of that family. She "bragged on" the successes of the team, not unlike a proud aunt, and honored the leadership and example of the coaches.[2] During the pastoral prayer she underscored the interdependence of family, teamwork, and community. In her sermon she spoke directly to the members of the team about the relationship of teamwork, the endurance of the love of God, and our own responsibility to endure in the tasks we share for the sake of the team, the church, or the community. During a reception with cake and punch following the service, Rev. Martha and other adults moved among the teen-agers, greeting them and sharing with them words of encouragement for the season ahead.

Other adults stood out on the lawn after the service discussing events of the week and commenting on the service and sermon. During the weeks that followed we heard numerous references to the importance of the congregation's involvement in the schools, to the significance of God's enduring love for people in and outside the church, and to the responsibility of Christians to endure in the tasks before them even when the challenge seems overwhelming. We heard no direct connection to this specific service of worship made in these comments. Instead, the themes simply seemed to come back into many conversations in a variety of settings. Rev. Martha often provided some theological or ethical grounding for the issues discussed in the conversations that followed. When the conversation lagged, she prompted them again in worship, business meetings, or other public settings.

Other persons however, were just as likely to initiate congregational conversations. One young African-American woman, for example, became increasingly interested in the need of older adults in the congregation and community (most of whom were European American) for day care. This interest motivated her to return to college to work on a masters degree to prepare herself for such a ministry. She made her concerns known during worship services. She talked with people of the church in many different places and a variety of times. Near the completion of her studies, the church asked her to present her proposal to a gathered assembly of people in the church. As usual, children and youth attended and participated in the discussion.

Elsewhere I have noted that congregational conversations contribute to the dynamics of learning in a congregation. The experience of mutuality among the participants requires a "willingness to suspend prior commitments and views" with the expectation they might undergo some change in understanding, relationship, or skill."[3] Conversation among Cedar Grove members, even during the extended discussions on the front lawn after the conclusion of worship services, conveys the interplay of candor and intimacy integral to this experience of mutuality. It may reach its most profound levels during the retreats for women and the all-night vigils of men preparing for the annual barbecue, where conversations often turn to deep sharing over issues of race, age, the quest to be faithful, and shared concerns about the well-being of the community. The collaborative character of these conversations, however, may be one of its most important educational features. Rev. Martha often initiates a conversation, prompts others to speak or act, and provides salient information to keep it going. In some respects she engages the congregation in conversation much as an orchestra conductor directs the interplay of musical instruments. But as in a musical score, others in the congregation may also initiate a theme in the conversation and help sustain it as it works its way through the life of the congregation.

The marginality of Cedar Grove may intensify the character of the conversations that shape and inform the congregation's common life. Members clearly recognize that what the congregation will become is not an obvious extension of its past. The racial diversity of the congregation sets it outside the mainstream of black and white church life in the South. The sense of urgency church members have about the well-being and future of both church and community underscores the necessity of their conversation.

A CURRICULUM
FOR CONGREGATIONAL IDENTITY AND VOCATION

Maria Harris, in an exploration of the meaning of curriculum, notes that in current usage it tends to be equated with "subject matter" or the content of teaching. This meaning has lost the intent in its Latin roots, *currere*, which means "to run." Harris suggests a return to its roots so that we might talk about the curriculum as the "entire course of the church's life" to be found in the way congregations and larger church communities fashion and refashion their integral forms and mission.[4] We have chosen to order our description of the ecclesial and educational dynamics in these congregations around this more active view of curriculum, which, as Harris points out, encompasses the priestly, prophetic, and political life of a faith community over time.

This returns us to the discussion of the "signs" we discovered in each congregation that evoke and order congregational relationships, traditions, images of identity and vocation, and structures. They illumine the distinctive course to be run in the fashioning of lifestyle and commitments integral to each congregation. In our discussion of Cedar Grove five signs seemed especially important in giving direction and meaning to the way its members understand themselves to be a community of faith and how they participate in the continuing task of fashioning that community for the future.

A Sign of Relationship: "We Are Family"

Undoubtedly the most explicit sign giving shape to Cedar Grove's identity and vocation is evoked in almost all public gatherings when Rev. Martha (or some other church leader) declares, "We are all family here." The meanings members of the research team brought to our hearing of the phrase were quickly shattered. It means, according to one African-American male leader, that "we eat in each other's homes all the time." Rev. Martha underscored the political overtones in that statement when she declared that eating the bread and drinking the juice of the eucharistic meal made her and an African-American youth sister and brother. Those words not only break racial boundaries by placing an African American and a European American in the same family, but they also break traditional hierarchical structures in churches and families by making a pastor and a youth sister and brother.

The language of family and family relations is deeply rooted in the life of the congregation. One of the founding families dominated the early history of the congregation. The church's membership has always included several generations within the same family units. That continues into the present, although most members of the younger generation of European-American families have left the community and most African-American families have not lived in the area long enough to establish a similar pattern. But certain members in the congregation take on traditional family roles for everyone. One European-American man, for example, has become Uncle Jody to almost everyone younger than his more than four-score years.

The dynamics of what it means to be family at Cedar Grove, however, is more evident in the way people relate to each other than in the language they use to describe those relationships. Small African-American children spontaneously hug older European-American men and women. Church members join an African-American layperson actively involved in the athletic programs of church and school and Rev. Martha to create a cheering section at local high school sporting events "to support our kids." Church leaders (black and white) brag about the accomplishments of children in the church like proud aunts and uncles. The matriarch of the Sri Lankan family oversees the church's after-school program on weekday afternoons in the church's gym and classroom building, as much a grandmother as teacher to the children involved. It is not unusual for a child whose parents are not in church to choose to sit beside her during worship. On Sunday mornings several adults—both black and white—often set boundaries for and discipline children to whom they have no blood relation. Sometimes this takes the form of direct verbal reprimands: "No running in the sanctuary," "Now quiet down you all!" Other times they are quiet reminders of appropriate behavior and language. A typical example occurred one Sunday morning prior to the worship service. One of the acolytes was instructing another acolyte on how to walk down the center aisle to light the candles on the communion table.[5] Their comments to each other became louder and louder until the two began to scuffle over the taper. An African-American woman stopped talking to a friend to intervene. With a few quiet words order was restored and she resumed her conversation.

Rev. Martha clearly serves as a grandmother or aunt for many children in the church (and as a sister to the adults). Children often "hang out" at her home or run to her in times of trouble. More than once children have declared in the heat of an argument with their parents they will leave to live with Rev. Martha, as if she were a favored aunt. Teen-agers stop by the house at almost any time during the day or night to talk.

In the declaration that "we eat in each other's homes all the time" we may discern a second dynamic in the way Cedar Grove views family. The people of Cedar Grove church *do* eat in each other's homes, but they also eat together at the church a lot. Family night suppers every month or so feature a rich variety of salads, vegetable dishes, and desserts along with the customary ham and turkey. A barbecue in the fall and spring begins with a group of men rising long before sunrise to begin the rituals of the cooking process. Church meals at Thanksgiving and other holidays and a concession stand during volleyball and basketball games in the church gym extend the list of times the congregation gathers to eat.

The gathering is at least as important as the eating. Before Sunday school a group of people slowly forms around the coffee pot in the kitchen. It took us a while to understand that when a fellowship supper was announced as beginning at 6:00 P.M., this meant people would *begin* to gather at that hour to set up the round dining tables, make the coffee, and organize the food tables. Discussion about children, church, and community punctuate the work. Since the church has no custodian, people gather to take up the chores of building maintenance, cleaning, and lawnmowing. There is also gathering after congregational events. After worship many people linger on the lawn in front of the church for thirty minutes and more. After church meetings and other activities people stay around to talk to each other. Members greet each other warmly in the store or on the street. Almost any occasion seems to provide an opportunity for socializing. These groups quickly form and slowly disperse, perhaps because the task at hand does not make up the primary agenda for their gathering. Instead, talking with each other takes priority.

For many people these times of gathering for eating, working, socializing, and meeting seem to be "just plain fun." Rev. Martha often sums up this feeling by declaring that "we have a lot of fun around here." But it also becomes evident as the Lord's Supper is served on the first Sunday of the month that a sense of sacredness permeates much of their gathering. During one meeting several members tried to describe for us the depths of their feelings for each other. Black and white men and women struggled to find words to talk about the mystery they experienced in their relationships with each other, but the tears in their eyes revealed the depths of those feelings.

The image of family communicated by this congregation is not the traditional, nuclear, middle class, American U.S. family. This family comprises people of differing cultural and racial backgrounds. It is headed by a woman who de-emphasizes hierarchy and role designations, refusing to wear liturgical garb, for instance, because it creates distance between pastor and people. People share responsibility for overseeing the children. It reminds one of the intergenerational character of the kinship networks of many black and white rural churches throughout the southern United States, but, in this instance, black and white members belong as brothers and sisters to the same family. It also resembles the African notion of the family as binding together the people of a village. When Cedar Grove folk talk about being family, however, the conversation centers on the primacy of their sense of relatedness to each other, the sense of intergenerational bonds of commitment across racial lines, and the shared concern for the well-being of the community in which they make their homes.

Caring for each other and enjoying each other's companionship day to day is close to the heart of what this community seems to be about. The vision of *koinonia* embodied in these words is not a principle to strive for. Rather, the vision of the church as family reveals the intimacy St. Paul envisioned for church fellowship, in which people's care for each other is not dependent on their status as men or women, Jew or Gentile, not based on age or race, but rather on their willingness to carry each other's burdens and to join together in celebrating the goodness of God.

A Sign of Action: Free in Christ: "We Just Do It"

Whereas the first sign centers on the identity of the Cedar Grove congregation, a second explores how the congregation works. Central to the way this community of faith "runs its course" is the leadership of its pastor. When Martha Forrest first came to Cedar Grove, some local business people were a bit skeptical—"her being a woman and all." Many members of the church shared these ambivalent feelings. After twelve years, however, vivid images dominate the comments of church members when they discuss Rev. Martha. One of the first African-American couples to join the church recalled the first time they met her. She came to their door on a Saturday morning—clad in a miniskirt and sporting large dangling earrings—to recruit children for the Sunday school. For another African-American young father she models Christian caring: "If there is a fire or some disaster, Rev. Martha will be the first one there, regardless of whether the people belong to the church or not." She will pick a child up at school if a parent gets in a bind, call a member to sing "happy birthday" before announcing who has called, or listen to the concerns of store clerks, school teachers, and teen-agers without regard for their relationship to the church.

Rev. Martha is bold and vivacious, nurturing and caring. She is also politically savvy, and local business leaders admire her keen business sense. She has no secretary and gives the impression that this arrangement suits her fine. "People know," she says, "how to get in touch with me." She claims to attend only the meetings she wants to attend, and she keeps no known schedule. Yet she is described as hardworking and dedicated. People agree she is available when needed. She often finds herself at odds with denominational officials—"the men downtown"—yet she has twice won grants from the denomination to help fund church projects, and twice she has been elected by her clergy peers to represent the North Georgia Annual Conference at the denomination's policy-making quadrennial General Conference.

Rev. Martha takes on the tasks before her with courage and conviction. Certain frequently repeated phrases establish standards and help motivate congregational life: "We're family together" articulates her assumption of the common bond that gives impetus to shared concerns; "Aren't we having fun?!" underscores her zeal for participating in the unfolding of God's work; "Isn't that great?!" announces her sense of growth of the extent to which a situation or relationship reveals the immanence of the kingdom of God.

Her son created a sign spelling out "Rev. Martha" for her office door in bold red and purple. In many respects it illumines the catalytic character of her leadership in the church and through the church in the larger community. Rev. Martha inspires a remarkable sense of boldness and confidence in and beyond the congregation. Early in her ministry, for example, she attended a basketball game being played in the gym of a nearby church and sensed the less than gracious reception for the black coach of the Cedar Grove team. At the next Wednesday night Bible study meeting she announced, "We're going to build a gym!" An 82-year-old retired contractor in the group immediately responded, "And I'll build it."

The congregation did not have the financial resources to build the gym. To build a gym when the future of the church was still precarious required a leap of faith. But they conducted a fund drive anyhow, sought and won a grant from the denomination, razed the old neighborhood schoolhouse (which some people still regret), and built a gym with classrooms and a large kitchen. In a similar spirit they bought a van, started an after-school program and summer camp for children, worked through the P.T.A. to reduce violence in the local schools, remodeled the sanctuary, fought efforts to rezone part of the neighborhood, and purchased a tract of land behind the church building for future expansion. When asked about conflict during these projects, little is remembered. This may be due in part to Rev. Martha's style of leadership, which focuses on building bridges, including everyone in the decision-making process, and remaining ever open to new ideas and new possibilities. She trusts the wisdom of the lay leadership of the congregation and will rarely make a decision without consulting those whose insight and experience will most effectively illumine an issue or problem. She makes sure that all issues have been "talked through" with black and white lay leaders. When members of the church come to her to obtain an opinion or judgment on some idea or proposal, she usually suggests that they "talk it over with some others." The implication is clear. Whoever initiates an idea is responsible for its review by church members.

At Cedar Grove literally anyone can initiate an idea, regardless of whether he or she is on a committee or in a leadership position, whether child or adult, male or female, black, white, or Sri Lankan. Significant ideas tend to arise in informal conversation in this church—often during a church supper or while visiting on the lawn after worship—and then take shape through public and interpersonal coalition building. On more than one occasion we saw Rev. Martha in the midst of a conversation at a table during a family night supper and then heard her exclaim, "I think that's a great idea!," and then, turning to those around her, "[Name] just said we ought to . . . I think that's a great idea, what do you think?" If others respond positively, the idea begins to gain support and will either gain or lose strength through more informal interpersonal discussion over the coming weeks. If it has sufficient support, or at least has some dedicated "cheerleaders," it will eventually be placed on the agenda of some meeting.

Typically, by the time an idea reaches a committee at Cedar Grove, it is well formulated and has garnered a significant constituency of advocates who will be willing to implement it. These advocates often seem only to need the sanction of a committee in order to carry out the idea. If any resistance to the idea is indicated during a committee or board meeting, the issue will likely be "tabled." Ideas are rarely rejected outright and tabled items often continue to develop or simmer informally, perhaps re-emerging in some modified form after having worked their way again through the informal channels of conversation.

Just like most newcomers to the church, it took some time before we could see this process for doing ministry at work. Every time we would ask how something had been done, answers tended to be vague. Board and committee meetings seldom lasted as much as an hour. They seemed to focus more on ratifying decisions rather than exploring issues. When pushed for more information about the congregation's way of engaging in ministry, the most common response we received was "we just do it."

These words increasingly signified for us the way things get done. Decisions to build the gym, buy the van and the land, and to start the after-school and summer-camp programs are prominent examples of what happens every day in this congregation. Parties, covered dish suppers, educational programs, even liturgical events seem to be conceived and scheduled instantaneously in casual conversation, with the details worked out later. Workdays to make repairs on the church building or to care for the church grounds can be organized one day and carried out the next. When people are inspired to do something, they "just do it." During one Council Board meeting one of the African-American women announced that the condition of the bathrooms near the sanctuary was an embarrassment and something needed to be done. A few days later in worship Rev. Martha announced the bathrooms near the sanctuary were being refurbished and a special collection was to be taken to help cover expenses. Through congregational conversations, in other words, a clear consensus had been reached. We gradually discovered that this style of decision-making is not simply a congregational pattern but is grounded in a theological commitment.

Rev. Martha believes her essential message as a pastor is to proclaim "freedom in Christ . . . free to be who we are . . . and to live as we are called to live." For her this freedom originates in the unconditional love of Christ, which honors every individual regardless of race, age, gender, or position as an eternally valuable child of God. This theme prevails in her preaching, teaching, interactions with people about church and community business, and in her evaluation of proposals for new directions in the life of the congregation.

Persons who belong to or interact with this community are automatically granted the dignifying status of "free, responsible, and valuable human being." Their ideas and perceptions are recognized as a legitimate part of the thoughts and perspectives of this community of people, and as such they are potentially useful to the entire community. And there is clearly a justifiable belief that this community of responsible persons is quite capable of implementing any ideas it judges worthwhile. They are "free" to "just do it."

This freedom, however, is balanced by two other dynamics in the life of the congregation. Freedom does not mean the license to do whatever someone might want. It is mediated first by a keen sense of responsibility for the well-being of the community and care for individual members.

A second dynamic became more evident to us during another worship service. After the prayer of confession Rev. Martha instructed the congregation to stand and greet each other with the words, "In the name of Christ you are forgiven." Children, youth, and adults, men and women, black, white, and Sri Lankan stood and moved around the room, solemnly proclaiming forgiveness to each other in the name of Christ. During the year, often in worship, but also during business meetings and social gatherings, Rev. Martha talked about the importance of forgiveness in sustaining community life or led the congregation in petitions for forgiveness. She described for us the importance of developing a climate of forgiveness in a culturally diverse congregation, because people do and say things that are not intended to frustrate, confuse, or hurt others, but in fact do so. The "freedom to just do it," in other words, is tempered by a sensitivity initiated by the pastor in a ritual act, but carried out in a general tolerance, often touched with a bit of humor, for cultural behaviors and perspectives that are not fully understood.

In summary, at least four sources contributing to the development of this pattern of leadership and decision-making in the congregation may be identified. Perhaps the most obvious centers on Rev. Martha's relational style of leadership and the value she places on collaboration, cooperation, and care in the way she works with others. Often associated with feminine perspectives on leadership and decision-making, her leadership style contrasts with those that emphasize the codification of procedures, the categorization of ideas, and the dynamics of confrontation, competition, and conquest in decision-making. Her quest for consensus and solidarity helps create an environment in which differences are not only honored but nurtured.

The "leisurely" sense of time often linked to agricultural cycles of planting and harvesting and the high commitment to interpersonal relationships often associated with small and rural churches (both white and black) in the South may be a second source to the distinctive patterns of leadership at Cedar Grove. Issues simmer over long periods of time as they are pursued, clarified, and tested through informal channels of communication.

The anti-hierarchical character of this approach to decision-making, moreover, may be one way this congregation continues to live out of its lay-centered Methodist Protestant church heritage. Longtime members are used to assuming leadership and responsibility for congregational life. Rev. Martha once said that the folks here "don't hold much to bishops and district superintendents. They don't care a whole lot about the system. They appreciate it, and they know how to use it, but they don't seem to get hung up on it." In other words, they "just do it."

A fourth source may be traced to the common quest for consensus in decision-making. This quest does not focus as much on finding something upon which all can agree as it does on seeking ways to include the concerns of everyone in a final decision. Strong leaders (black and white) nurture the dialogue of the constituency during worship, business meetings, and informal conversations in the church and throughout the community. Everyone is not only permitted but encouraged to participate in these conversations, to give evidence of support and dissent in building a decision. Through this process, a decision not only carries the willingness of the people to accept an action, but it gathers up and reformulates the collective wisdom of the congregation. Attention centers on developing rather than making a decision. The Cedar Grove preference for collaboration, cooperation, and caring fits well in and is influenced by this tradition, which is deeply rooted in the religious heritage of African Americans and the experience of both white and black extended families.

A Generational Sign: Jesus and the Children

The central window along the side of the sanctuary depicts Jesus and four children—two with light and two with dark complexions. This affirmation of children seems to signify another value in the life of Cedar Grove. Children and youth are not only visibly present, but their voices are taken seriously. Adults seem to gather children into their arms and lives as a matter of course. We have already noted that children participate actively in the worship, fellowship, and business life of the congregation. When asked about their willingness to listen to the voices of the young people in church, several adults responded by claiming that the freedom of young people to speak their minds helps "keep us honest."

Congregational concern for children extends to advocacy and caretaking roles for many adults and the congregation as a whole. The after-school and summer-camp programs were organized to provide a safe place for children of working parents in the community. The Cedar Grove tradition of active involvement in the Parent Teachers Association and other school organizations as advocates of children and youth continues through the work of current members. Service on these committees is perceived to be as important as any role of leadership in the church. Church members proudly identify the six or seven members who have served as presidents of the P.T.A. and others who have earned lifetime memberships in the organization. Their involvement moves beyond the support of school officials and programs to advocating for the safety, well-being, and quality of the education children in the community are receiving. When school discipline became a serious problem, for example, church members working through the P.T.A. proposed and supported a dress code for the school. Men in the congregation concerned about the lack of adequate role models for African-American male youth sponsor events where these young people have the opportunity to meet outstanding African-American male leaders in the city.

The dynamics of caring are also evident in the ways in which adults praise, set boundaries, and discipline children who are not their own.[6] It is seen in the number of adults whom children spontaneously seek out to hug in the midst of their play. The concern for children prompts some adult members to teach Sunday school, others to lead scout troops, coach basketball and volleyball teams, provide transportation or organize parties. Those who feel they are too old for direct leadership can always be counted on to provide cookies and other baked goods for various activities. Young people are attended to, cared for, nurtured, and respected in this church to an unusual extent. When asked about their expectations of these mostly African-American young people during a congregational meeting, several European-American adult members asserted that "they will be the leaders of this church and community." A teacher in the local school added that it is easy to spot Cedar Grove children at the school where she works because they move easily back and forth between white and black students and faculty. This concern for their future is reflected in the affirmation of the value of the after-school program, where the tutorial support the participating children receive has raised most children's academic performance at least one letter grade. There is a conscious assumption at work in this church regarding the importance of the encouragement and support of all adult members if the young people of the congregation are to live into their expectations for them.

A Sign of Social Action: "Community" Church

For most of its history Cedar Grove United Methodist Church stood at the center of the life of the larger community. In the mid-1970s the membership of the church reclaimed that place and in the 1980s, with Rev. Martha's leadership, reclaimed responsibility for the quality and character of public life in the community. In a sense church members concur with John Coleman's assessment that responsible citizenship in the community for Christians depends on congregations which first induct their members "into a vigorous community of memory whose special and particular memory is that of disciples who follow the practices of Jesus."[7] Cedar Grove takes this responsibility seriously.

Rev. Martha keeps an attentive ear tuned to the "goings on" of the community. On a typical day she stops at the local "five and dime" to chat with the owner or cashier, perhaps about plans for a parade, last evening's high school football game, or the weather. She stops regularly at the barber/beauty shop and picks up a diet coke at the convenience store across from the church. She moves on to the high school, where she jogs on the track and talks to some of the staff. On these rounds she finds out the news of the community, who is sick, and how the county commissioners are attending to community needs. She knows all the local business people well and they know her. Most are not members of the church, but she is an informal counselor and confessor and does some weddings and funerals for them. She became involved in the local P.T.A. and continues to be an officer of that organization and her neighborhood association.

While Rev. Martha may be the community listening post, the activists in the church's ministry in the community are found among the members of the church. Over the years many of the school board and P.T.A. officers have come from the church. Key people provide visible and consistent leadership to the church's volleyball program, which draws people from a large part of the county. The gym, while giving young people a healthy place to "hang out," is considered by some of the local business people "what makes it safe to walk the streets at night."

The gym is the local polling precinct and the gathering place when politicians and others seek to address the larger community. A number of church members are active in local civic organizations and consciously seek to influence legislation that reflects their Christian values. Other members are teachers, staff members, coaches, or students in the dominant community organizations—the local public schools. Most church members perceive their membership in and commitment to the church and community as being very much intertwined. Sunday morning announcements and prayers are just as likely to include mention of the high school football team and local zoning ordinances as the recent church youth activities, plans for Lent, or names of people in the hospital. Community leadership responsibilities are weighed carefully when nominations for church offices are made. Several younger African-American members trace the impetus for their own active involvement in the community to the influence of the church.

An important difference, however, must be noted between the community leadership provided by the contemporary Cedar Grove members and that of church members before 1950. The church and the society used to meld together into a common sense of community. That is no longer the case. When the demographic composition of the community changed, its institutions for the most part became isolated and declining enclaves maintained by long time residents—many returning to the community only to worship or meet old friends. Most African-American residents maintained their ties to churches and organizations in the city.

The difference became evident to us during a family night supper called to help us sketch out the history of the congregation. One member noted that in the midst of this disruption of their community, members of the church finally realized they "were the only ones who could stabilize this community." That realization proved to be a turning point in the congregation's history. It led church leaders to assume responsibility for bringing stability to a community experiencing rapid growth and racial tension. That effort contributed at the same time to a new sense of purpose and mission for the congregation.

The task of stabilizing the community did not involve attempts to protect the congregation from the changes surrounding it. Rather, it focused on recreating a caring community to encompass racial and cultural diversity. The first step in this process involved achieving a sense of this new community among themselves. The arrival of Rev. Martha gave direction to this effort. Church members began reaching out to each other and to those moving into the community to form a culturally diverse but interdependent and caring community. In so doing, church members consciously witnessed to the community that black and white can live together as brothers and sisters.

The gym extended the scope of the congregation's effort to stabilize the community. Once built, the gym quickly became a focal point—a gathering place—for an even more diverse racial and cultural constituency. Thus the community, of which the church was (and is) the center, expanded to take in much of the southern part of the county. This, combined with the conscious attempts of church leaders to move out into community agencies to influence school policy and local legislation as a means of advocating for children and promoting racial harmony, served (and serves) to make the church a prominent and powerful stabilizing and transforming force in its community.

A Sign of Difference:
"We're Special But They Don't Understand Us"

Into this sign may be gathered much of the ambiguity Cedar Grove members experience about the public role and responsibility they have assumed. Cedar Grove is unusual in a number of ways. Most visible is the multiracial/multicultural composition of its membership. On a Sunday morning one sees both dark-skinned and light-skinned persons in the pews. The "style" of the church (its way of worshiping, fellowshipping, governing, and educating) reflects traditions rooted in both European and African cultures. Its style is also influenced and informed by women and men, elderly persons, young working professionals, children and youth. Those who look in from the outside find it difficult to find appropriate categories to comprehend what they see. It is not a black church and it is not a white church. The governing structure is not hierarchical, but its lay and clergy leadership are strong and visionary. Although it has experienced considerable change over the past ten years, it conveys a sense of vitality and energy. And yet, it is not clear what kind of church it is becoming. Will it become a *black* church like others in the area? As the city continues to expand can it continue to be the spiritual and moral *center of the community*? All this means that Cedar Grove is not well understood by other churches in the area or by its own denominational officials.

Perhaps this lack of understanding may be summed up in the response of a denominational official about Rev. Martha's long tenure: "Who else could we find who would know how to serve this congregation?" A year later, when the bishop did appoint her to another church, he also asked her for suggestions of persons who might be ready to follow her. In effect, contrary to United Methodist practice, Rev. Martha helped to name her own successor. Ambivalence about Cedar Grove may also be heard when church leaders and pastors hold up Cedar Grove as an ideal for church life but have no idea about how to begin to create such a congregation. Perhaps it is most evident in the words of a black clergyman who wondered how a white woman preacher "could attract so many black members," or in the words of several white clergy colleagues who wondered why a preacher would want to stay in such a congregation. These statements are received as backhanded compliments. They underscore a consciousness that Cedar Grove breaks traditional norms for congregational life. For the most part, this breaking of boundaries and exploring of new frontiers excites Cedar Grove members. They reinforce, at the same time, a feeling of isolation which both frustrates and strengthens their commitment to each other as "sisters and brothers in the Cedar Grove family."

The experience of ambivalence takes other forms as well. When a research team member asked the chair of the Council Board why he stayed at Cedar Grove Church he responded quickly, "I don't believe in church hopping." His words reminded us of an African-American football coach's observation that one of the crucial sources of Cedar Grove's vitality was to be found in the stubbornness of some of its white members. This was not just plain reactive stubbornness, but a stubbornness directed toward the goal of "being church" in the midst of a changing community.

The presence of stubborn persistence, however, can also be found among the black membership of the church. The first African Americans joined the congregation even though it seemed "awfully white" at first. They continued to "hang in there" even though the worship and life of the church contrasted at many points with their prior experience. "We don't come because of the singing," said one member. "We come because we happen to be family together."

The larger Cedar Grove community has undergone significant change during the past twenty years. Subdivisions have replaced dairy farms. The neighborhood school has given way to large regional schools. The population used to be mostly white and is now mostly black. Cedar Grove Church has felt these changes profoundly but has resolutely stood its ground, persisted in its ministry, and in recent years has experienced growth in membership and influence. The long history of service of the church to the community persists in new forms and through new people. Perhaps the Council Board chairperson put it best. When asked to predict what might happen when the dynamic Rev. Martha leaves, the response was: "Ministers come and go, but the church remains."

In exploring sources to patterns of ambivalence in the life of the church, however, perhaps the most deeply ingrained is at the same time one of the most distinctive strengths of this congregation: its challenge to the racial dynamics of the deep south. For anyone familiar with church life in Atlanta, certainly one of the first things to be noticed on visiting Cedar Grove is the significant presence of both white and black members. And yet deeply rooted social attitudes about the relationships of white and black in the larger society both intrude upon and create an agenda for the congregation.

One of the stories we heard from several people recalled an incident early in Rev. Martha's ministry at Cedar Grove Church. A death occurred in the family of one the first black families to join the church. The wife of the man who died requested that he be buried in the church cemetery, which is administered by a separate board of trustees. This request meant he would probably be the first black person to be buried in the cemetery since the nineteenth century. A white woman in the community tried to block the widow's request. When Rev. Martha approached one of the cemetery trustees, he observed that if the board did not meet to discuss the matter the funeral could go on as requested. He concluded by noting that if the church were to be integrated, he guessed the cemetery could as well. The move beyond integration, however, to the transformation of deeply rooted racial perspectives does not come easily. A prominent member of the church and strong advocate of the congregation's life and ministry made this point when Rev. Martha asked him: "Are you still a racist?" After a long pause, he answered with a thoughtful tone to his voice, "Not as much as I used to be."

The issue of race cuts both ways. Some black visitors do not return to the church because its pastor is white and a woman. Many of its members are white. The church does not feel like a black church to them. When a group of Cedar Grove children visited a black congregation, several wanted to know why the preacher shouted so much. Some parents wondered later if by choosing Cedar Grove they were depriving their children of an adequate exposure to black cultural experience. Black members taking leadership for the first time experience some awkwardness in their new position with white members. White members anxiously wonder what will happen if the bishop appoints an African American to be their next pastor. Their apprehension was heightened after a nearby congregation received its first black pastor who, shortly thereafter, wrote a letter to its white members urging them to transfer their membership because the church was "now black."

At the same time, the constant negotiations that occur between black and white members of Cedar Grove do point to some new possibilities for race relations if churches take their example seriously. Promise can be seen in the collaboration of church members over any issue or program they address. It can be seen in the willing participation of several black members in a choir directed by a white man, more out of their appreciation for the care this man shows than his ability to introduce black church music into the life of the church. It can be seen in the increased consciousness of white members to the racism permeating the church and other institutions in the larger society. It can also be seen in the observation of members of the church who are around the schools a lot regarding the ability of the children of Cedar Grove to move back and forth between black and white peers and teachers. They seem to have an unusual facility to interact in a bi-cultural manner. Since the population of the Cedar Grove community is overwhelmingly black, demographic projections do not reinforce a long-range vision for a culturally diverse congregation unless church members seek to work in new ways at that task. That issue will become a major agenda item for the congregation and its new pastoral leader.

Notes

1. I previously had explored the role of conversation in congregational education (Charles R. Foster, "Communicating: Informal Conversation in the Congregation's Education," in *Congregations: Their Power to Form and Transform*, ed. C. Ellis Nelson [Atlanta: John Knox Press, 1988], 218-37). In that essay I had assumed that informal conversation in congregational life often provides a kind of infrastructure giving credence to and supporting the formal schooling patterns in the congregation's education. In the Cedar Grove Church we discovered something quite different. Informal conversation was integral to the teaching and learning patterns of the congregation.

2. At the end of the season the church not only rented a bus to give church members an opportunity to attend an important league play-off game; it invited the team back to be honored both during the worship service and a reception that followed.

3. Foster, "Communicating," 226.

4. Maria Harris, *Fashion Me a People: Curriculum in the Church* (San Francisco: Harper & Row, 1989), 55, 63-64.

5. In this incident we see illustrated the involvement of children and youth and the supervisory role of adults in the transmissive teaching practices of the congregation. The youth with knowledge and/or experience in a given situation instructs another, who will soon share the responsibilities. This pattern is, of course, a common one in families in which older siblings are responsible for the instruction of younger ones into many of the values, habits, attitudes, and practices considered important to the maintenance and renewal of family life.

6. Nel Noddings makes an important distinction between *caring* and *caretaking*. The former involves an action "with special regard for the particular person in a concrete situation." It is not motivated by the desire for commendation but "to protect or enhance the welfare of the cared-for." In contrast to the "nonrational and subjective" dynamics of caring, caretaking involves a more rational and objective approach to the care of someone. The danger, Noddings emphasizes, among groups who approach human

needs out of the more abstract notion of caretaking that "something must be done" is to redirect the caring act to problem solving. This was not the dominant pattern at Cedar Grove. Caring responses involved direct and immediate acts for the one to be cared for (Nel Noddings, *Caring: A Feminine Approach to Ethics and Moral Education* [Berkeley: University of California Press, 1984], 24-25).

7. For an extended discussion of the relationship of a pedagogy for citizenship and discipleship, see John A. Coleman, "The Two Pedagogies: Discipleship and Citizenship," in *Education for Citizenship and Discipleship*, ed. Mary C. Boys (New York: The Pilgrim Press, 1989), 54ff.

3

OAKHURST PRESBYTERIAN CHURCH

INTRODUCTION

It is cold and dreary, not the deep cold of a northern winter, just the grating dampness of January in Georgia. A rare snow has deteriorated into city slush and puddles, which my two preschool daughters and I step over and around as we cross the parking lot to enter a back door of Oakhurst Presbyterian Church early one Sunday morning. We move through two sets of doors into a back corridor that is nearly as damp and gray as outside. Variously referred to as a fortress, a castle, or an albatross, the building which houses this church is large, imposing, and deteriorating. From the street one sees a sprawling brick structure, located in a predominantly African-American blue-collar neighborhood where there is obviously little time and money available for the upkeep of many of the houses and yards. From the back one enters an education building meant to provide generous space for a membership of nine hundred in the early 1960s, including a second-floor recreation room, a spacious fellowship hall, offices, and a dozen classrooms.

Wending our way through the cinder-block hallways we pass signs and posters belonging to the Headstart program, which occupies five rooms on the first floor. The walls need paint, the floors are dingy, and there is a slight aroma of mildew or "old building." I have been visiting here occasionally for six months and have had a formal tour of the building, but I still do not know where that back staircase leads. A Girl's Club rents space somewhere on the second floor. An adult-literacy program uses the room at the end of the corridor in front of us. We turn down another corridor, passing a Sunday school room and nursery. The nursery serves as a day-care center during the week for children born with drug addictions. Climbing a short flight of wide stairs and turning left then right, we enter the fellowship hall. It is 9:00 A.M., and we are gathering for a breakfast and Sunday school program in celebration of the life of Martin Luther King, Jr.

In its own way the fellowship hall is warm and inviting. It has a thirty-year-old tile floor, but the cinder-block walls are freshly painted and some colorful posters on a free-standing bulletin board alongside another bulletin board display individual pictures of all church members. We smell coffee and sausages. The breakfast was "advertised" to begin at nine, but only four or five others have arrived ahead of us, and they are making last-minute preparations for the Sunday school program to follow the meal. I browse the members' board as my daughters explore the room. Approximately half the members of this congregation are white (45 percent according to a March 1992 membership report) and half black (54 percent). There are a few Hispanic and Native American members. The membership numbers around 140 and is slowly climbing from a low of eighty in 1982.

This has been a troubled church in a troubled neighborhood. An urban renewal program in the 1960s displaced large numbers of black folks from their downtown Atlanta homes, initiating a rapid transition in this peripheral neighborhood as many sought affordable housing just outside the city limits. Formerly white, working class, and suburban, the neighborhood was becoming an integrated extension of the inner city during the 1960s and 1970s. The Civil Rights Movement was very real here; Martin Luther King's Ebenezer Baptist church is less than two miles away. Following Brown *vs*. Board of Education the public schools were integrated, and many white folks fled the neighborhood, causing membership to plummet in this congregation—from nine hundred to eighty in fewer than twenty years. Those who stayed or joined in the late 1960s and early 1970s found themselves struggling for survival in an unstable neighborhood. Their legacy from the past included an aging building meant to provide space for the religious and social life of nearly one thousand comfortable white folk, as well as a concern among some members for social justice and race relations. In 1958 the congregation's pastor participated in a city wide race relations summit and signed a Racial Interdependence Manifesto, which was published in the local newspapers. In 1972, just two years after the first African American became a member, the congregation, with an all-white Session called a black man to be pastor. He soon became the denomination's first black moderator.

This commitment to racial integration and justice has strengthened and deepened, and has begun to bear fruit over the past ten years. In 1983 the congregation called Gibson "Nibs" Stroupe to be its pastor. Nibs is conscious of being a white man from the South whose life was changed by his recognition as a young man in the 1960s of the thorough-going racism in U.S. society, in his own family and friends, and in himself.

This recognition of a system of racism in the church and nation continues to characterize Nibs's basic orientation to the world and, increasingly, provides the impetus to Oakhurst's ministry. The existence of racism as a central structuring theme in U.S. society is a primary teaching in this congregation. As one member puts it, "Oakhurst is at times a one-issue church—race relations—and some cite this as they leave. But the race issue is our map of the world; it is not an isolated issue, but a part of being. It is a metaphor for brokenness." This understanding leads Oakhurst to view itself as a consciously counter-cultural community. Its members understand racism as a primary ordering influence in society—a part of who we are. At the same time, the members of the church consciously order their lives around being racially diverse and inclusive.[1]

With his ordained spouse, Caroline Leach, and two small children, Nibs brought a deep commitment to fostering genuine cultural diversity in this church and ultimately to "overcoming the barriers which separate us." In his preaching, teaching, counseling, and everyday conversations, Nibs consistently proclaims "God has made us one in Jesus Christ" and "nothing can separate us from the love of God." One leader in the church, an African-American woman, says the thing which made her stay with the church is "the basic foundation of a sense of justice. Every day we are here we are reminded that there is not anything that can separate us from God." For Nibs and Caroline, their sense that humans are called to relationship with God and each other through Jesus Christ translates into a vocation of relationship building. They have worked hard and skillfully at breaking down walls and serving as translators, mediators, and reconcilers between persons of African and European decent both in the congregation and in the community, as well as between the community and the governmental agencies that have an impact upon the community's life. There is now approximately even representation of African Americans and European Americans, women and men among the lay leaders of the church. And the congregation's service to and influence in the community is extensive.

"Good morning Ted; good to see you!" Nibs greets me from behind and offers a comment on the breakfast getting a late start, "We're on CPT this morning, and folks really aren't used to getting out this early on Sunday anyway." CPT is "colored people's time," an expression used playfully by both white and black members to signal the relatively low value given to punctuality in black culture compared to the relatively high value on punctuality in WASP culture. Because it exists as an inside joke, the expression serves to diffuse tensions which linger, and perhaps will always be present, due to differing cultural expectations about time. (We found this practice of finding humor in the paradoxes and conflicting expectations associated with the co-existence of multiple realities to be common in all three congregations of this study.)

Since Nibs's style of dress contrasts sharply with that of most black pastors, jokes are made about this as well. Nibs is a plain-looking man in his mid-forties with a twinkle in his eyes. He is five feet four inches and trim, but one cannot imagine him enjoying jogging. He dresses as though clothes are far from his mind when he gets up in the morning, sometimes wearing a tie and sometimes not, sometimes slacks and sometimes jeans, sometimes shoes and sometimes sneakers. Clearly he marched in the 1960s and is still marching.

Caroline, Nibs's spouse and Oakhurst's associate pastor, greets us also. Caroline is strikingly friendly in this setting. For the most part, I have seen and heard of Caroline before primarily in her capacity as minister of outreach: challenging the status quo at school board meetings; taking commissioners to task for feeble and discriminating housing policies; advocating for the community health center, drug addicted children, illiterate adults, low income parents. This morning she is not carrying those burdens. She seems excited and buoyant. She is delighted to meet my family and eager to make us comfortable.

The Martin Luther King breakfast is a time for celebration in this congregation—it is a "holi-day," a "feast day." In the words of Victor Turner, it is an experience of "communitas."[2] We are introduced to a few other people. My daughters become instant hand-holding friends with the visiting niece of an African-American member. Children can feel the mood and know how to revel in it.

By 9:15 Nibs calls the twenty or so people present into a circle for prayer. Before every event in this church joys and concerns are shared and people gather in prayer. A congregant's mother died last week; some people have been burdened by the weather; thankfulness is expressed for our being together this morning, and for the life of Dr. Martin Luther King, Jr., in whose honor we are gathered. Hands join—young and old, black and white, a seminary student, a mother on welfare, a garage mechanic, a retired professor, a postal worker, a physician—and hearts unite in prayer. The people share a commitment and dream: a commitment to make this counter-cultural community of diversity work; and a dream that one day they will not be counter-cultural, that unity and justice among all persons will prevail. But they are eminently realistic. They proclaim that in Jesus Christ "the dividing walls of hostility are broken down." Yet they see walls constantly being erected and re-erected in "the world." The walls must be dealt with everywhere every day.

After the prayer we move toward the table laid out with foods hinting at the variety of cultural influences in this congregation: dry cereal, fried apples, quartered fresh apples, banana halves, muffins, breads, scrambled eggs, sausages, corn bread, grits, and more. Food provides an opportunity for a visible and enjoyable celebration of cultural diversity. But it also can make the cultural differences tangibly and uncomfortably clear. Some say this congregation used to have a breakfast nearly every Sunday prepared by a few older white women who "controlled the kitchen." But black members found their "traditional" breakfast fare unappetizing. So they changed to the present "dish to pass" format. But then black folk started bringing "stuff that just didn't seem like breakfast food at all" to some white folk. Interest in the community breakfasts faded. Cross-cultural collaboration in the kitchen was also tried; this led to a scene many recall as both humorous and illustrative of the tension. One African-American woman burst out laughing in the kitchen one morning when a long-standing white member tried to advise her on how to cook grits: "She's gonna show me how to make grits? Does she know we've been making grits for generations? Does she know we taught her grandparents how to make grits?" Collaboration in the kitchen still happens, but the dish-to-pass format prevails—allowing for genuine diversity and the expression of cultural specificity.

About fifty people show up this Sunday by the time the meal is over. Nearly a third of them are children who will constitute the first half of the program (followed by a lecture—with children and youth still present—on the legacy of the Civil Rights Movement by a black professor from a nearby interdenominational seminary). The children's and youth's Sunday school classes have been preparing for this program for weeks—memorizing songs or lines from speeches, making posters or banners, learning about Frederick Douglass and Sojourner Truth as well as Malcolm X and Martin Luther King.

As the eating winds down Nibs raises his voice to ask for everyone's attention so that Caroline can make a presentation. The Citizen of the Year Award, we are told, is presented each year at the Martin Luther King breakfast to recognize a member of the congregation for his or her outstanding contributions in the local community. The recipient this year is a recent member who works in the day care. She is an African-American woman with children in grade school and a husband whose salary is quite modest. It became clear to me in a subsequent interview that she experiences this congregation as a remarkably supportive and loving family of faith. "We're just like a big family here. . . . Everyone helps each other out." Some members who can afford to do so take her children shopping and to the movies. She calls these gestures acts of "amazing love, and not charity, since we're all in the same family." She takes her responsibilities in the day care very seriously—it is her role in this family and her ministry to the community she lives in. She is silent and clearly moved as she accepts this recognition award.

The elder who oversees the Christian education ministries is introduced next. Inez Fleming is a vibrant middle-aged African-American woman, and a rising lay leader in this congregation. She is not shy about helping Nibs see where and when he might delegate some more responsibility. Nibs acknowledges quite frankly that when he came to this church "power had to be taken away from some white folks who were holding all the power; they were willing to let black folks in, but not willing to let them lead." He has slowly been redistributing that power over the past ten years by encouraging African Americans to take leadership positions. But the time has now come for the membership, both black and white, to take on new levels of responsibility. The congregation must not be so thoroughly dependent on its pastoral staff to broker all its internal relationships and to ensure its future. Inez and Nibs seem most consciously aware of this. Inez is clearly in charge of this program now. She introduces each Sunday school class and invites each class in turn to come forward and share what its members have prepared. There is art work, memorized paragraphs from African-American history books, and songs.

The recitation of part of King's "I Have a Dream" speech by junior high youth stands out as particularly powerful, moving many, including me, nearly to tears. Overall, about 75 percent of the chil-

dren in this congregation are African American, with only a few
European Americans among the senior highs. But the junior highs,
given leadership by a middle-aged European-American husband and
wife, are fairly well mixed—four European Americans and five African Americans on this particular occasion. Many members see this
group as a test case. At this age they remain relatively innocent of
the charged racial/sexual dynamics of black-white relations in our
society. Will the church be able to "keep them together" into their
senior high years? Will the white teens fade away as they or their
parents become uncomfortable with cross-cultural dating? Will the
African-American boys find it necessary to "act out" in resistance to
white authority here in the church, as elsewhere in society? Can this
congregation's experience of culturally diverse communitas be "passed
on" to its young people, or must they (youth and adults) continue to
participate in constructing the "dividing walls of hostility" before
they can experience the grace of having those walls dismantled? This
morning, here in the heart of Georgia, with their bellies full after a
generous and diverse breakfast, this mixed group of emerging ado-
lescents stands together and declares with determination and conviction:

> I have a dream that one day . . . on the red hills of Georgia the
> sons of former slaves and the sons of former slave holders will
> be able to sit down at the table of fellowship together. I have a
> dream . . . that my four little children will one day live in a
> nation where they will be judged not by the color of their skin
> but the content of their character . . . and one day right down
> in Alabama, little black boys and girls will be able to join hands
> with little white boys and girls as sisters and brothers. I have a
> dream. . . . [3]

THE LEARNING COMMUNITY

The neighborhood in which this church is located, once all white,
now has a black majority. Though the immediate neighborhood is
comprised of modest single unit dwellings, a nearby apartment complex has a reputation for drugs, violence, and civil neglect. The
congregation's outreach to addicted infants (through day care), at-
risk children (in the Headstart program), illiterate adults (through
the adult-literacy program), and needy persons of all ages (through
a "clothes closet") conveys clearly that, as its mission statement puts

it, this is "a church in the city." Although members come from many parts of the city, inner-city problems surround and help define this church. Some members do live in the immediate neighborhood. They tend to be black and may work as hairdressers or mechanics or teacher's aids. More members drive several miles to attend. They are both black and white, both professional and working class—a geologist, a lawyer, a medical-school administrator, a department-store clerk, a public-school teacher, a receptionist. Another significant contingent of members and affiliates has some formal ecclesial connection—students and professors from a nearby Presbyterian seminary, persons having formerly served as missionaries or presently on leave, a director of an ecumenical Christian council, an official in the denomination's national staff, a pastoral counselor. Eight ordained ministers from among the congregation assisted with communion one Sunday morning during our study (all white, seven male).

Overwhelmingly, those who attend this church do so out of a serious commitment to social justice and racial harmony. This small church has a big mission. It therefore demands a lot from its members. As one member put it, "This church will drain you dry if you're not careful; it is a young person's church—you need drive and energy to be a member." Another member articulated succinctly the sense of urgency and mission that seems to "drive" many members; "This church is needed to heal the wounds of racism." This member was thinking primarily of the church's functions as witness, advocate, and prophet in and beyond its city.

Many members also come to this church for the healing of their own wounds. They include families of mixed race or differing religious affiliations, gay or lesbian persons or couples, and others not readily accepted in the mainstream of U.S. society (or in many other mainline churches). Some also come here in an effort to reconcile their own Christian faith with their disillusionment over the church's participation in racism and segregation, its support of an unjust status quo, its sheepishness about controversial social issues, and its internal preservation and perpetuation of patriarchal structures of hierarchy and control. Some African-American women are very clear that they "could never go back to a black church" because they would not be able to hold similar leadership and decision-making positions. Others value "the freedom to be ourselves," which they find here. One European-American man from this congregation recalled that he rebelled during his college years against the church telling him what to think and believe. He remained disillusioned with the church's stance on social issues during his early adult years. When he moved to Atlanta and began looking for a church to attend with his small children, he found this church to be a place where he could feel connected and accepted. They welcomed him "with open arms" without requiring him to conform to their ways of thinking first—"I was OK with them, so I figured they were OK with me too."[4]

This non-traditional church appeals to a wide variety of people discontented with traditional church—whether that "tradition" is black or white, Baptist or Presbyterian. People come because they want the diversity and the exposure to differences. They want to participate in challenging the status quo, but they also need the support this community provides as they engage in this struggle. Perhaps because they are acutely uncomfortable in other settings, most members accept some level of discomfort here as part of the character of genuine diversity. No one is entirely at home here. This is a white church, and a black church; it is a Presbyterian church, with Baptist and Pentecostal influences; its ministries are oriented toward social justice concerns; its stance is theologically evangelical, and liberal. An occasional advertisement in the church section of the local newspaper reads "Multi-racial, forward-thinking, biblically-based, Jesus-centered," and that is a fair description. Some social justice activists like the church but cannot bring themselves to join because its theological assumptions are too explicit. Some members of the congregation are uncomfortable with the way the church reaches out to homosexuals or advocates feminism or allows spontaneous expressions of faith during the worship service. There is something here to offend everyone; there is also something here to include everyone. Such is the character of this church. As the mission statement puts it:

> We are a community of diversities. We come from different places, from different economic levels, from different countries of the world. . . . We are young woven with old, black with white, male with female. We are employed woven with unemployed, poor with comfortable, strong with broken. . . . These differences are the threads that the love of Jesus Christ weaves into the one tapestry—Oakhurst Presbyterian Church.

This community of diversities is "woven into a single tapestry." And, both explicitly and implicitly—in word and in action—in these "weavings" learning happens most powerfully. As people join hands for prayer before a social event, for example, one of the community's orienting teachings is both spoken and enacted: "In Jesus Christ the dividing walls of hostility are broken down and we are made one people, one family, brothers and sisters in Christ." Or again, as the community gathers for worship, the message is heard from the pulpit: "The world tries to define us and tell us who we are—black, white, rich, poor, straight, gay—but the gospel tells us we are all children of God."

The weavings and not the formalized teachings seem to embody the actual curriculum of this community. Unless they are in preparation for some special event, the teachers of children in the Sunday school struggle to keep their efforts from becoming dry and strained as they attempt to do what teachers "are supposed to do": transmit relevant and important knowledge to their students. But compared to the meaning-filled creative weavings of church-wide events, these efforts seem anemic. Talking about the good news is far less powerful than experiencing it; discussing the overcoming of barriers and the freedom to be found in Christ is more difficult in this culturally diverse church than actually doing it.

The annual Christmas pageant we witnessed is a good example of the powerful learning found in congregational events. During the potluck supper preceding the Christmas pageant there are clues of the event and the weavings to follow. The table decorations recall traditional European Christmas themes—paper evergreen trees, holly leaves with red berries, white snowflakes. But there are also indications of the African-American celebration of Kwanzaa—a three-foot leafless tree branch adorned with black paper ornaments shaped like people, red triangles, and green squares. Each ornament lists a gift suggestion—personal clothing items, a talent to be shared, something for the kitchen or a Sunday school room. The pageant is structured in the style of the Poseda, the Mexican-American pilgrimage to the birthplace of the Christ child. The evening is introduced by one of the congregation's ordained affiliate members, a European-American man who serves the metropolitan ecumenical council as executive director. The decorations are explained, guests are introduced and welcomed, and a prayer is offered. Among the dozen or so guests is an African-American pastor of a nearby Pentecostal church, who informed us that he holds this church and its pastor in high regard. After the meal the congregation migrates from the fellowship hall to the sanctuary directly above.

The sanctuary was painted less than two years ago in contemporary pastels—colors that picked up and highlighted the stained-glass windows. A high ceiling arches over the old wooden pews, which seat perhaps three hundred. Stained-glass windows punctuate the sides of the room. At the front of the sanctuary one's eyes are drawn to a large stained glass window above the raised choir loft. The window portrays Jesus towering above a gathering of disciples. A few years ago the skin tones on Jesus and some of the disciples were changed from light to dark. This decision made some people, both black and white, uncomfortable (the window had been donated by an older white person who had since left the church but still lived in the area). However, it was the unanimous decision of the Session to change the window, and the congregation quickly adjusted to it. It is now only visitors who seem to notice the dark-skinned-Jesus overseeing the sanctuary. A white Jesus remains in a smaller stained glass window over the balcony in the rear of the room. This evening the sanctuary is decorated sparingly with greens, banners, stars, and angels. As it fills with the buzz of focused activity, the room feels friendly and cozy, though the congregation will, as usual, take up no more than half of the pew space.

The pageant has never been rehearsed completely. Indeed, only a few of the scenes have been rehearsed at all. Nonetheless, more than sixty persons of all ages and from several cultural backgrounds are prepared to participate. And, prepared or not, the rest of the gathered congregation will also participate. A European-American woman from the congregation who has planned and organized the event greets the congregation from the front and makes sure all planned participants are present. She replaces a reader who has not arrived and gives some brief final instructions.

The pageant begins with the congregation singing "O Come, All Ye Faithful," followed by a drum roll and trumpet fanfare, readings from Isaiah, and visits from angels to Mary (an African-American teen) and Joseph (a European-American seminary student). As the holy couple process down the center aisle toward Bethlehem, they are preceded by two women—one playing a zither, the other a recorder. A troupe of children follow singing the Hispanic carol "A-la-rue." Senior high teens standing in the pews with signs indicating various inns turn the couple away as they approach. Mary and Joseph "register" at a table at the front, followed by the procession of children, and then everyone present ("all the world") files forward to register as well.

When the shepherds (played by three African American and two European-American mid-high youth) are "blinded by a bright light" from the angels, two whip out sunglasses to shade their eyes. In the next scene three teens (two African American and one Hispanic) perform a simple liturgical dance during a reading from Luke about the alleluias of the heavenly hosts and while a solo voice sings "Joy, Joy, Joy." Seven "wise leaders"—men and women, young and old, dressed in street clothes, African festival clothes, and bright robes—carry gifts wrapped in satin-looking cloth. They move slowly down the center aisle while an African-American woman sings "Rise up, Christians, and Follow." The gifts are presented at the manger and their satin streamers attached to a hidden banner. When the banner is finally lifted, several gasps of awe are heard. A white dove stands out against a black backdrop with the satin streamers waving boldly below. The congregation joins in singing "We Shall Overcome . . . (We shall love each other . . . we shall live in peace)" followed by "Go Tell It on the Mountain," "O Little Town of Bethlehem," and "Silent Night." Joy to the World" concludes the evening.

This event illuminates well the character of this congregation's life and the sort of contexts in which that life flourishes. Several aspects of the event are worth noting. First, the event was centrally planned and coordinated. Though the director consulted with others along the way, she had primary responsibility for the event. We witnessed a similar pattern throughout the life of the church. A single person or small committee (of two or three) is often given, or takes up, responsibility for a project. While six or seven people arise repeatedly as leaders, such responsibilities are fairly well distributed, with no one having pervasive "control" over church life. Yet the person responsible for any given event is not really "in control." There were no full rehearsals for the pageant. Costumes were completely left to the discretion of each participant. People were invited to participate who never rehearsed at all, and ad-libbing was common (witness the shepherds with sunglasses). With a mixture of planned action and spontaneity at work in each event in the congregation, the outcome is really unknown. People enter into the experience with anticipation that something exciting and something good is unfolding, but with little control over the final product. We heard the choir sing "There Is a Sweet, Sweet Spirit in This Place" repeatedly as its introit; the people of this church have come to trust that spirit.

The semi-impromptu Christmas pageant evolved in response to tensions surrounding the exclusion of children who had not attended a sufficient number of rehearsals. We were told that the first time the new pageant was enacted a young unwed African-American mother assumed the role of Mary. Having been told to wear whatever seemed appropriate, she showed up late for the performance wearing jeans, T-shirt, red socks, and sneakers. A "biblical looking" headpiece was added by the director and the production went on. No one was sure what would happen, but according to several witnesses "the kids really got into it." "Their imaginations took over." "They were spellbound at the manger scene and did not want to leave." The director overheard someone comment that "the kids knew what they saw up there." This mixture of planned action and free-flowing spontaneity is risky. Some events disappoint people. But this risk-taking also results at times in moving experiences of God's grace.

Similar risks are taken in Sunday worship. A feeling of Presbyterian decency and order sets the tone for the service. Within that structural framework congregants also have experiences of "anti-structure." About midway in the service Nibs leaves the chancel to march up the middle aisle toward the center of the sanctuary, where he stands midway between the stained-glass windows with the dark and light images of Jesus. There he invites congregants to share joys and concerns. Anyone may stand and say whatever he or she wants—for as long as he or she wants. Some do not just say it. One elderly African-American woman occasionally moves to the center aisle and Nibs slowly takes a seat while she sings her witness—a soulful solo on the joys or burden (or both) of life and faith. Most of the joys and concerns are personal and fairly brief, though details are considered important. But occasionally sharings become sermonettes, lectures, or apparent performances. Once a lawyer lectured on the Bill of Rights for nearly ten minutes. The ordination of some elders one Sunday prompted a startlingly dramatic solo song and tribute to the newly ordained. Some quietly complain about how long some people "go on" at times, but Nibs persists in allowing complete freedom of expression here, or at least in not discriminating among expressions. (When he feels truly restricted by time, he asks for all sharings to be written on slips of paper provided in the bulletin and then collected by ushers.) Even those who complain seem not to question Nibs's right to let it "go on." Nibs admits he is sometimes uncomfortable when too many sharings are long. But he takes it all in stride, affirming and reiterating and contextualizing whatever comes.

Nibs has an astounding memory. He can weave fifteen or twenty joys and concerns into an all-inclusive pastoral prayer—without notes. But it is the contextualizing of each prayer request that is so powerful and so pedagogically significant. Immediately after a concern is shared Nibs repeats the concern for the rest of the congregation, points out its theological or social significance, and sometimes relates it to other concerns of the congregation. After all have shared, he groups the sharings around theological and social themes in his pastoral prayer, framing everything in terms of human sinfulness and divine grace. It becomes clear when Nibs leads the congregation in prayer that, for these folk, God is active in this world and the details of their lives are all ultimately meaningful and important.

WHO TEACHES AND THE CHARACTER OF TEACHING

The experience of an older African-American member of the church illustrates something of the character of teaching in this congregation. This retired postmaster had attended black Baptist churches most of his life. Five or six years ago he married an African-American Presbyterian woman and started attending Oakhurst with her. He is now an active member of the church and of the Friendmakers Sunday school class.

Leadership for this class rotates among its members. Sometimes the class decides together on a topic for discussion and then an appropriate teacher from among them will emerge to lead the discussion. Other times class members take turns and a topic is found to fit the interests of teacher and class. Including the pastor, at least four regulars in this class possess an M.Div. degree. Two hold church-related doctorates. Capable discussion leaders and participants are always ready at hand. As this retired postmaster put it on this particular morning, "It certainly is wonderful to have all these scholars around. . . . They enlighten us and give us things to think about." But the comment feels awkward following his nervous statement that he is "supposed to be the teacher" this Sunday but is not really prepared. Soon he defers to Nibs for guidance, saying, "We don't really know what we're doing." Nibs takes over as teacher this morning by leading a discussion on his sermon text for the day. When Nibs returns the leadership to the designated teacher toward the end of the class period, he instructs the class to choose a topic for the next two or three weeks. The retired postmaster suggests they focus on the "women of the Bible." Over the next couple of weeks he takes an increasingly active leadership role, initiating questions and facilitating discussion among those more "scholarly" than he.

In some ways this vignette can be seen as a metaphor for the character of teaching in this congregation. This layman is not the only one who feels "unprepared" and senses that "we don't really know what were doing here." And it is not only this same man who, with a little encouragement, takes up the responsibility to "lead the way"—sometime with trepidation, sometimes with boldness.

A middle-aged European-American couple leads the junior high youth group. The group is about 60 percent African American and 40 percent European American, and thus poised to become the congregation's first effectively integrated group of senior highs. The dynamics which press toward segregation in this age group are complex—residual racism among parents emerging at the prospect of interracial dating, the growing consciousness of racial identity, a need for racial solidarity (especially among black male youth), growing peer pressure to conform to common (segregated) race-relating patterns, and the prevalence of racially segregated high schools in the city. Although adults in this church have chosen to work against prevailing social attitudes toward race, the challenge of bringing the church's message of "being one in Christ" to life among its senior highs has not yet been fully met.

This group of junior highs seems promising to the congregation. They are active, upbeat, and have developed important friendships across racial lines. The adult leaders are praised for their "wonderful work with that group." But these apparently effective youth leaders say that they don't know what they are doing or how to keep doing it. Indeed, they feel the group is so precarious they urged us not to observe any of their meetings as researchers. Nonetheless, they move ahead with hope, doing the best they can, noting that "at least it's exciting."

Most of the children's Sunday school teachers share this sense of excitement, anxiety—and insecurity. Differing assumptions and expectations regarding the conduct of Sunday school among European-American and African-American teachers and students intensify their questions about the role and purpose of the Sunday school. In many cases teachers begin to question their own assumptions about what it means to teach and to learn, as well as their assumptions about the tradition they seek to teach. What do these students need to know? What is the best way to retain control in the classroom? Am I supposed to be in control? What does control mean? The presence of real diversity in this congregation means differing responses to such questions, and the high level of consciousness regarding this diversity and relativism means it takes real courage to teach. As one member put it when talking about the constant threat of misunderstandings due to differing expectations and assumptions, "I finally decided I would go ahead and offend people—it cannot be avoided unless I just don't say anything—and then try to patch things up afterward." In other words, while she realizes that she cannot master any situation sufficiently to understand all of the various cultural meanings others might attach to it, she cares too much about those others to remain silent. She speaks at the risk of offense and teaches in the face of her own ignorance, but that willingness to speak and to teach is born of care. This congregation understands the gospel to have a similarly bold and offensive character.

CURRICULUM AND METHOD

As previously indicated, we have come to view our research as story collecting. We have clustered our collected stories around a series of "signs" in an effort to make collective/generalized meaning of the stories and to gain a composite view of the congregation as a whole. Finally, we understand these signs as the functional curriculum of the congregation—they point to and name what we, the researchers, see as the prominent teachings of the congregation. In other words, the stories that cluster around these signs embody the deeply held goals and messages of the congregation, which the signs seek to articulate. Four signs organize our understandings of Oakhurst Church.

A Sign of the Times: Racism Is on the Rise

"We are in a time of rising racism. Oppression and injustice in our culture are growing, especially in regards to black people." This statement, made during a Sunday sermon and later distributed at the request of the Session in manuscript form to friends beyond the congregation,[5] articulates a repeated and prominent theme at Oakhurst Church. In various forms it can be heard from the pulpit, in Sunday school classes, and in casual conversations; it is printed in newsletters, occasional letters from the pastor to the editors of local newspapers, and in circulated sermons. This is an explicit and primary part of the curriculum in this congregation.

As the Christian message of the good news of redemption only makes sense and is good news if one understands the bad news of human sinfulness, so the good news of racial harmony and equity at Oakhurst Church (as well as its prophetic voice of justice in the wider community) only makes sense and is good news if one understands the bad news of racism. Drawing on current events, the history of the Civil Rights Movement, and the ongoing personal experiences of members, the reality of racism is addressed and illuminated continuously in this congregation. David Duke and Pat Buchanan, the Los

Angles riots, Anita Hill and Clarence Thomas, Ida B. Wells and Nat
Turner, a member's recent confrontation with the judge of a local
grand jury over racist practices in the courtroom, the inequity of
funding in the city schools . . . all of these are "texts" that embody
this central teaching—racism is on the rise.

Two aspects of this basic teaching are worth noting. First, it directly conflicts with the modernist myth of progress that dominates
much of Western culture. During the time we studied this congregation, Nibs was working on a book drawing parallels between what
he saw as "the re-establishment of slavery in the 1890s" and the
rising racism of the 1990s. In other words, we have not moved ahead
but have come back around to the same old issue and our same old
patterns. Second, some people have left this church in recent years
citing the relentless emphasis on racism as tiresome and depressing,
and some who remain shared with us their periodic frustration about
this being "a one-issue church." Furthermore, it is not coincidental
that those who did express this frustration were white males—who
find themselves consistently implicated by the way the issue is articulated. However, the clarity of this issue lends, at the same time,
coherence and focus to the diversity of persons and concerns in the
congregation.

The mission of the church moves well beyond the task of naming
the issues of racism and social injustice. The congregation houses
and supports a Headstart program and an adult-literacy program. It
reaches out to youth in a nearby housing project. Members work in
community centers, halfway houses, and with a homeless ministry.
Letters are written to national legislatures, local newspapers, and
neighboring churches. A community health center is supported. The
associate pastor participates boldly in local political processes in
behalf of the congregation. The ongoing witness of the congregation's
very existence as a racially diverse community of faith in an environment of racial tensions both attracts and repels people in the neighborhood and city. The impetus for such action comes from the
congregation's awareness not only of the bad news of racism, for
alone that provides no hope (and hopelessness does sometimes haunt
members), but also of the good news of Jesus Christ.

A Sign of Hope: The Good News of Jesus Christ

"For he is our peace, who has made us both one, and has broken
down the dividing wall of hostility" (Eph 2:14, paraphrased). This
passage from Paul's letter to the Ephesians is ever present in the con-

sciousness of this community, and almost always follows in some form after any reminder of the bad news of racism. The peace and oneness of Christ are experienced as the congregation gathers together every Sunday for worship, in fellowship around meal tables, in their work together maintaining the building (they have no paid janitor or maintenance staff), and in serving the community. But for many members such experiences are not repeated outside the church community. The power of race (and the "dividing wall") is seen and felt as real and definitive "in the world." The breaking of the walls is thus a prophetic cry—a call to repentance and to action. "Breaking" is not a gentle metaphor. Nibs once sent a card table, which had been standing curiously near the pulpit, crashing down the chancel steps during a sermon on the cleansing of the Temple. During our study some Oakhurst members picketed a nearby Presbyterian church on several Sunday mornings to protest a new policy it had adopted regarding the use of its property by homeless persons. There is a clear consciousness that, as they say, "the powers and principalities of this world" need to be boldly confronted.

The good news, however, is not entirely a call to confrontation for them. They are also acutely aware of the presence of Christ in their neighbors. As they open their clothes closet to the needy, provide food to a community center, welcome people unconditionally into their fellowship, provide support to a community health center, and advocate for some imprisoned black men and decry the racism in the penal system, the text from Matthew is never far from mind: "I was hungry and you gave me food . . . a stranger and you welcomed me . . . naked and you gave me clothing . . . sick and you took care of me . . . in prison and you visited me" (Mt 25:35-36, NRSV).

No matter how little effect it may have, no matter if racism is rising and the powers and principalities seem to be prevailing, this congregation is committed to mediating the presence of Christ in their world. That commitment is fueled by the glimpses of hope and new life they experience when the walls are down in their midst. One retired European-American couple, both very active members of Oakhurst Church, told of their long-term relationship with what they refer to as a "subpar income family" composed of an African-American woman, her now-grown children, and her brother. They have given their time and money and energy to this family for fifteen years, advocating for them in court and with utility companies, employers, landlords, and prison wardens. Yet the family's situation remains fundamentally unchanged; "they are always on the verge of eviction . . . always facing some crisis." The powers and principalities—the structures of race and class and gender in our society—often seem unmoved by the efforts of these earnest and caring mediators. Still, they keep up the struggle, driven on in significant part by their experience at Oakhurst— their hearing and experiencing of the good news prevailing over the bad news, at least at times, at least in this small community of faith.

A Sign of Humility: We Are All Children of God.

Another important part of the curriculum of this congregation is signified in the phrase "we are all children of God." As their mission statement makes clear, they are "young and old, black and white, employed and unemployed, poor and comfortable, strong and broken." This is the vision and experience of life without dividing walls. "There is lots of love here!" declares one member in an effort to explain what makes this congregation work. "Its like a big family reunion" says another, describing fellowship dinners.

Perhaps many congregations speak of themselves as a family, but this message that "we are all children of God" differs from most family rhetoric. Whereas the notion of family can imply a rigid and unjust hierarchical structure, the notion that we are all children implies a degree of parity among persons and a shared experience of being "childlike."[6] This common experience of being childlike points to the prevalent feeling in this congregation that no one is really in control, even while they take on significant responsibilities. Rather, their life together seems to unfold in ways that cannot be determined in advance. They are not experienced parents guiding others along; they are all eager and ever learning children.

Two aspects, then, of being "children of God" as this congregation understands it are 1) that no one person or group is in charge (serving as the socializing parent), rather, everyone is seen as relatively naive and inexperienced; and 2) the future is seen as unfolding out of the collective interacting of the members of the family, rather than being decided by "parents" or leaders.

A Sign of Beauty: Weaving the Rainbow Tapestry

One manifestation of the pluralism in this community is that a plurality of metaphors for communal self-understanding exists, with no one metaphor being clearly dominant. Thus, alongside the family metaphor of children of God is the crafting metaphor of weaving.

"The work of our ministry guides our diverse peoples to weave the fabric that is our tapestry" reads part of their mission statement. This weaving can be seen throughout the congregation. Banners suggesting diverse cultures often adorn the sanctuary. A bulletin board in the fellowship hall displays the diverse faces of the congregation. For several months a large multicolored rainbow adorned a nearby bulletin board intended to promote intercultural experiences. The six bands of the rainbow were labeled "Appearance," "Language," "Family," "Religion," "Homes," "Food." Comments written within the bands included "try something from Bangladesh" (in the food band) and "tolerance" (in the religion band).

The Christmas pageant weaves together Christmas, Kwanzaa, and Poseda celebrations, as well as ancient texts and contemporary life. African and European heritages are woven together in fellowship dinners. Persons can be seen dressed along the spectrum from business suits to sweat suits on any given Sunday morning. Whereas the broader culture often experiences diversity as problematic—leading to conflict and adversity—diversity is everywhere woven together in this congregation and is celebrated as beautiful, artistic, creative.

If the bad news of racism is the primary teaching and beginning point in this community, then "weaving together the rainbow tapestry" is the ultimate teaching; this is what must be done to overcome racism. Given the bad news that racism is real and rising, and given the good news that Jesus Christ breaks down walls of division and hostility and calls us all together as children of God, what we must do, proclaims Oakhurst Church, is weave ourselves together. And so they weave, as best they can, their lives, experiences, and traditions, in the hope and faith that something beautiful and something good will come of it.

SUMMARY

This congregation is a community of deep commitment, and profound faith. Its members are committed to being together and working together while differences remain in place. They are committed to being together and working for justice in a world where the "powers and principalities" of injustice are strong. They are driven by deep faith: faith that God is benevolent and that we are all children of that God; faith (like that of the well-loved child) that the future is worth living into; faith (like that of the joyful artist) that the work at hand is a work that needs to be done and is an expression of some creative power both within and beyond us. There is an openness to an ambiguous future here, and a willingness to risk comfort and security in the present in order to live in dynamic relationship with actual "others." This is a genuine community, with real diversity and profound faith—a culturally diverse community of faith.

Notes

1. Nibs Stroupe tells the story of his own growing consciousness of racism in the United States and the effect it has on the way churches communicate the gospel in *While We Run This Race: Confronting the Power of Racism in a Southern Church*. Written with Inez Fleming (an African-American layperson in the Oakhurst congregation) during a sabbatical granted by the congregation, the book explores the congregation's efforts to challenge the system of racism in the church and community (Maryknoll, NY: Orbis Books, 1995).

2. Victor Turner, *The Ritual Process: Structure and Anti-Structure* (Ithaca, NY: Cornell Paperbacks, 1969), 96-97.

3. The teacher of this class, an African-American woman, used a transcription of King's speech in rehearsing the young people for this recitation. The source of that transcription is not known. We used a video tape to transcribe this section of the speech ourselves (Home Video, Martin Luther King: "I Have a Dream," MPI, 1986). While Caroline or Nibs probably would have changed "sons" and "brotherhood" in the text to include female referents, no one seemed to be offended by hearing these words quoted from King's 1963 speech.

4. This quote is transcribed from an interview with this Oakhurst member by Ted Clark during a report on "Returning to Organized Religion," on National Public Radio's *All Things Considered* (April 10, 1994).

5. Included among these friends, and perhaps the primary intended recipient of this particular sermon distribution, was a nearby Presbyterian church that Oakhurst members were picketing in protest of its new policy regarding the use of its property by homeless persons.

6. For discussion of the theological significance of being "childlike," see Charles Foster, *Teaching in the Community of Faith* (Nashville: Abingdon Press, 1982), chap. 3.

4

NORTHWOODS
UNITED METHODIST CHURCH

INTRODUCTION

In 1955 a student from Candler School of Theology canvassed a new suburban neighborhood near Atlanta to discern interest in developing a new congregation. Ten people from this rapidly growing European-American neighborhood responded to his initial invitation to meet in the City Hall. A congregation formed, grew rapidly, and was officially chartered in January 1956. One of the developers of the neighborhood donated property across the street from a large park around which the neighborhood was being built. The first unit, which includes the present fellowship hall, was completed in 1961. It stood at the center of the neighborhood, providing a convenient gathering place for residents. People who lived outside the subdivision, however, often had difficulty finding it.

The new congregation developed a reputation for being friendly and open to visitors and newcomers. Adult Sunday school classes established strong fellowship groups, two of which continue into the present. An active women's organization embraced denominational study programs and outreach projects. As the children of church members reached adolescence, a vital youth ministry attracted young people across the community. In 1970 church membership passed four hundred. With space at a premium for church activities and parking, property to the south of the church building was purchased and an architect hired to design a new sanctuary. He proposed and the congregation approved an octagonal building designed to gather the worshiping congregation around a central altar/table.[1] The congregation's membership peaked at 711 in 1977. Nothing in the boomtown rhetoric accompanying Atlanta's rapid growth or in the assumptions about church growth among denominational leaders prepared church members for the years to follow.

Except for the details, the general outline of the next fifteen years at Northwoods paralleled the experience of Oakhurst and Cedar Grove churches. Changes in the neighborhood precipitated changes in the church. These changes became increasingly evident in the Northwoods community and church during the 1980s. The metropolitan region continued to expand to the north and east. Commercial ventures filled the houses along the major streets around the neighborhood. Turnover in the shops of the small strip-malls increased. Children grew up and left home for college and work. The average age of residents increased. Eventually the DeKalb County School system closed the elementary school down the street. Expanding personal incomes for many Northwoods families made it possible for them to move into larger homes in newer subdivisions. Many of their former homes became rentals. Some drove back to the church, but many joined congregations near their new homes.

The lack of a neighborhood school diminished the attractiveness of the neighborhood to younger European-American families looking for their first home. Apartment complexes built on the edges of the neighborhood and along the freeways attracted new immigrant families as well as African Americans and Hispanics with limited financial resources. Immigrants, especially from Central and South America, Asia, the Caribbean, and Africa who had begun to establish themselves financially began to rent or buy in the neighborhood. The congregation, which had served as the social and spiritual center for many young European-American families in the neighborhood, faced a crisis of identity and mission. By 1990 the number of Asian residents in the area had increased by more than 250 percent and the Hispanic population more than 150 percent. More than twenty-five languages were spoken among residents within a five mile area. The region had become the most ethnically diverse in the state.[2]

By 1988 church membership had declined to 284. Earl Brewer, a retired sociology of religion professor at Emory commissioned by denominational officials to study the future of the church, predicted it could not survive beyond 1992 at the current rate of membership attrition. Some in the congregation watched the changes and urged the congregation to work harder to stave off that threat. Visitation programs in the neighborhood did not result in many new members.

The Staff Parish Committee unsuccessfully requested permission from the North Georgia Annual Conference to reduce the salary of the pastor so the congregation could work within its actual income.[3] When a proposal was made to disband the youth fellowship due to the inability to find adult leadership during a church board meeting, a member in his seventies volunteered his services and, in what several described as a very emotional moment, declared the future of the church depended on its commitment to youth. Others shared his conviction that Northwoods did have a future. By refinancing the mortgage on the church and digging deeper into their own pockets to support the congregation and its ministry, they bought some time to make their case.

In retrospect, several clues to the future they were about to choose can be identified. Perhaps one of the most important can be traced back to the extensive involvement of Northwoods women in denominational women's programs of study and mission. As one woman reported, "The most subversive organizations in the South have been United Methodist women and Baptist women's groups," whose active support of improved race relations has "done the most to change southern society." Although overstated perhaps, her comment may point to one of the sources for the intense and deep commitment of many of the leaders in the United Methodist Women to the idea of a church that would welcome "the world at the doorstep of the church." Among the first to cross that doorstep was an older Liberian woman who discovered the church building on a walk around the corner from the home where she and her son's family had recently moved. She returned home to announce to her family that she "did not want to drive downtown to church anymore." So she, her Ethiopian-Italian daughter-in-law, and her grandchildren began attending.

In May 1990 the church hired Winston Worrell, an ordained Methodist pastor from Barbados and student in Candler School of Theology's doctor of ministry program, to be its youth minister. Some say the pastor hired him as an act of spite prior to his moving to a new appointment in June. Others say the church hired him to let its new neighbors know they would be welcome. Whatever the reason, the congregation, perhaps surprising itself, enthusiastically embraced Worrell and his family.

One month after hiring Worrell, the bishop of North Georgia appointed Jerome Hamm pastor of Northwoods. As Jerome tells the story, during the previous thirty years he had served congregations in small towns across Georgia and Alabama. Northwoods would be his first urban appointment. That alone felt daunting. As he drove down Buford Highway on his first visit to the church, he realized he was entering a "strange land." Nothing in his south Alabama European sharecropper heritage or prior ministry experience had prepared him for this community. Everywhere he looked he saw signs over shops and restaurants in Korean, Chinese, Spanish, and Vietnamese. The next Sunday morning (in a congregation that included Winston and his wife, the Liberian family, and a Mexican-American family who had come with a long-time church member), he compared the modern Atlanta to the vision of the Holy City depicted in Revelation 7. Both, he noted, included "all tribes, tongues, and nations." In Atlanta, "people gather to make money. In the Holy City, people gather to praise God." He posed for them the possibility that God was calling Northwoods to embody for Atlanta that vision of diversity in praising God.

For some long-time members that sermon kindled hope for the future of the congregation. During the next year Pastor Jerome, as many members call him, continued to describe through his preaching and teaching a vision of community drawn from New Testament narratives that celebrate diversity. In his exploration of that theme, he repeatedly returned to Revelation 7 to hold up an alternative image for the church. He became increasingly explicit about his own rural Alabama cultural roots and invited church members to identify and claim their own cultural heritages. Long-time members began to talk about where they had come from, including Pennsylvania, Oklahoma, most southern states, Panama, Italy, Germany, England, and Canada. Two more Liberian families and a woman from Jamaica began to attend. One of the new families joined. Within months after the Hamms had settled into the Northwoods community, the congregation's Administrative Council voted to become "a multicultural congregation," trusting that in the future they might discover what this action would entail.[4]

A clue to the implications of that decision occurred during the summer of 1991. A Mexican-American woman and her three sons joined the church. She joined the choir and became part of a new adult Sunday school class for younger adults. One Sunday morning she sang "How Great Thou Art" as a solo during worship—first in English and then in Spanish. Developing a sense of community across different languages no longer seemed quite so threatening to some. But it did to others. European-American church members continued to leave. By November of 1990 (within months after Jerome Hamm's sermon about the possibility of a multicultural vision for the congregation) membership dropped to a low of 242. New members, many from other cultural groups, soon offset the numerical but not the financial losses the church was experiencing. A year later the membership had rebounded to 299, but the financial crisis of meeting monthly bills persisted.

During the ensuing months the pastor and lay leaders began to explore what becoming *multicultural* might mean. They first focused their attention on the growing Korean community. Denominational officials, however, reminded them of two nearby Korean United Methodist congregations. However, a new proposal to start up a ministry among Spanish-speaking people did receive judicatory blessing and financial assistance. A Puerto Rican couple seeking to become lay pastors began to participate in the life of the congregation with the expectation they would be appointed to the church as leaders in that ministry. As this study ended they were approved and officially appointed part-time to the church. The initial direction for this ministry involved separate English and Spanish worship services, bilingual services four times a year on Sunday mornings and for special events, a single Sunday school and administrative structure, and a shared pastoral ministry. Even as the Administrative Council made this decision, new members with Caribbean, African, European, and Korean heritages continued to become members.

THE TEACHING AND LEARNING COMMUNITY

The Northwoods Church sits a short distance from the intersection of Interstate 85, which bisects the city, and Interstate 285, which circles it. When approaching the church from the former, one drives past an apartment complex with a predominantly Spanish-speaking population, a motel identified by a sign in Korean, and a row of small ranch-style duplexes mostly filled with young Hispanic men. These give way to small tract homes now filled with Korean doctors and shops. A small United Methodist Church sign points into the Northwoods subdivision. One turns a block later onto a seven-lane street. It runs past small shopping malls with older stores owned by European Americans and shops and restaurants directed to Korean, Chinese, Vietnamese, Indian, and Mexican populations. A small sign points into the subdivision behind the shops to the church. The street circles to the right past small brick and wood tract homes. Eventually the street winds past a park and the church. As we listened to long-time members of the church talk about their experience of the neighborhood while their children were growing up, we heard a shared sense of loss for the interdependence of the church, the neighborhood families, and the elementary school in the social and educational life of the community. Those families who remain continue to talk about their love of their home and community but seem unclear about how to contribute to shaping its future. Nothing in the community provides a common outlet for their concern about the quality of life in the community (as the school used to do). Those who moved away but return for church are also ambivalent. Their loyalty is to the church and no longer to the community, which is so different from their memories. Most of the newer members—European American as well as Hispanic, Liberian, and everything else—do not live in the immediate community. Some drive up to forty miles from their homes.

In the past the boundaries between the responsibilities of church, family, school, and neighborhood tended to blur for many in the church. It made little difference whether one was United Methodist, Baptist, Presbyterian, or Lutheran (the churches in the community), because shared values and cultural assumptions reinforced a sense of interdependence in the tasks of maintaining and renewing the life of the community. The current lack of clarity among church members about the church's relationship to the neighborhood is compounded by the scattering of its membership across a significant part of the city. Set in the middle of a sub-division, the congregation is no longer a neighborhood church. It has few direct ties to local political and economic life. Nothing in its history or its recent struggle to survive has prepared it to identify itself as a congregation with a regional or metropolitan parish. The result is an ambivalence about such basic matters in congregational life as when to schedule meetings and social events and with what agencies and institutions outside the church to be allied.

A sense of ambiguity, however, does not permeate the sense of place that embraces both oldtimer and newcomer *in* the church. Repeatedly people told us they "love this place." In it many claimed they "feel closer to God and to each other." The building provides a dramatic setting for the gathering of the congregation. The roof reaches high into the sky. Sidewalks from lower and upper parking lots follow the hillside to meet at the main entrance near but beneath the level of the street. At this point outside space closes in; the entry is of human dimensions. Entrance into the narthex, however, reverses that feeling. The clear windows opening up to the trees outside the church, the high ceiling, the warm, soft tones of the paneled walls, and a glimpse into the even more expansive sanctuary invite one into a place of warmth and awe. This space and the activities that take place in it may be the most forceful dynamic in shaping the way this congregation views itself and its mission.

When the people of Northwoods gather to worship they face each other. The attention of a person visiting the congregation for the first time is immediately drawn to the communion table at the center of the room, then to the large cross with intersecting crossbeams hanging over it, and on up to the illuminated stained-glass skylight above. The natural wood walls and pews convey the sense that this dramatic setting for worship is both hospitable and intimate—even when only half full. Many long-time members point to an informal Christmas eve carol service and a Maundy Thursday communion service as events intensifying the transformative power of this place in their lives.

In comparison with our visits to other United Methodist churches in the area, the worship at Northwoods tends to be quite liturgical. An earlier pastor introduced into their worship sung responses and the reading of the weekly lectionary, patterns of worship Jerome gratefully continued. A procession of robed choir and pastors circles the table as the candles are lighted and the processional cross and the Bible are put in place by youth or young-adult acolytes. From week to week Winston gradually rotates the place around the table where he calls the children to him for a story or conversation. Members of the church come out of their pews to take turns reading the various scripture lessons for the day. People gather at the kneeling rail, interspersing black, white, and brown persons around the table the first Sunday of each month for communion—an event that many identify as the high point in the rhythm of their worship life—and at the conclusion of each service of worship as Jerome calls people to prayers for the "church and world." New members gather around the table to be taken into membership, surrounded by church members who agree to sponsor their incorporation into the congregation's life. Those to be married come to the table to sign the certificate of marriage. Flowers or food are sometimes brought to the communion railing. And prayer services and vigils are held there during special seasons of the year.

Jerome makes dramatic use of the space as he preaches "from the table" rather than the pulpit—pacing and gesturing, roaming the dais and sometimes the sanctuary, circling the table, looking into the eyes of congregants and reminding them as they see each other across the room that the cross and table both center and bind them into community. The implicit message becomes explicit: Northwoods is a community called from all over the city and world to gather around the table at the foot of the cross. It is a community nurtured by word, sacrament, and prayer.

Movement around the cross and table establishes the rhythm for the concentric circles that move the Northwoods congregation out into the larger community. Each Sunday following the sermon and the morning offering Jerome invites the congregation to gather around the cross and table to "pray for the world." As many as can fit kneel at the communion rail around the table. Others stand behind them forming a larger circle that spills over into the aisles and pews behind them. The prayers led by Jerome move through a litany of intercession for specific people, institutions, and issues in local, metropolitan, state, national, and global situations. Time is provided for people to call aloud or identify in silence the names of persons or issues for which they have a special concern or are especially thankful. After these prayers conclude, Jerome instructs the people to take each other's hands so they might experience the bonds of reciting together the Lord's Prayer. The benediction is then pronounced and the people are urged to greet their neighbors with "a handshake, a hug, or a kiss"—which some do with considerable enthusiasm. Many linger in that room centered by the cross and table to talk. As we began the study, most of the small groups that formed tended to be divided along ethnic lines. As we approached the conclusion of the study, these conversations had begun to move across those lines.

The shape that gathering around the cross and table gives to the life of the congregation extends beyond the sanctuary. At the end of the Sunday school hour each class gathers into a circle to link hands for prayer. A similar prayer circle forms around the tables in the fellowship hall prior to a community meal. A circle forms at the end of meetings to gather the community in prayer. The image of the community gathered around the cross and table also spins outward into the larger community in concentric circles. It encompasses such congregational efforts as working with the homeless, supporting programs for children with special needs, and helping in a variety of ways to assist the denomination's urban ministries program.

Each week, as the people of the congregation gather around the cross and table, Jerome reminds them in some way that they are "the people of God" and "near to the heart of God." Gathered "from all over the world," an increasing number see in their common life a vision for community beyond the congregation. The struggles integral to forming that community, however, become more explicit as one moves out of the sanctuary into the educational wing of the church.

Large classrooms, sturdy tables and chairs appropriate to the age group, bulletin boards, and a supply room still organized according to a system instituted almost twenty years ago indicate that the members of this church have a long-standing commitment to education—in school and in church. That commitment persists for some, but it has been severely tested. Only a few newcomers sporadically visit the traditional adult classes. Jerome started a new class for young adults and a large and diverse group gathered each Sunday—as long as Jerome continued to be its teacher. Bonds of fellowship existed more through his presence than with each other. In contrast, youth with backgrounds in several nations developed close ties with each other under the supervision of their Sunday school teacher and Winston. Sitting together during the worship service—Liberian, European American, Thai, Mexican American, Caribbean, and African American—they provided a regular reminder of what a diverse community might look like.

New members, especially those who spoke Spanish, brought their children to Sunday school. Many of the Liberian children attended if church members gave them rides. The number of children's classes increased from one to four. Noise in the halls indicated renewed vitality in the church. But teacher frustrations illumined the difficulty of creating a culturally diverse congregation. Some children would arrive thirty to forty minutes after the sessions had begun. Teachers who looked at their teaching as a sequence of learning activities found it difficult to accommodate these "interruptions." Lack of English language skills among the younger children tested teachers' communication skills and patience. Tensions reached a crisis point in the preschool class when teachers tried to figure out a way to prevent one of the Spanish-speaking boys from pinching other children on the cheeks. Teachers initially viewed this as a hostile act on the part of the child until one saw his father greet him that way after the Sunday school session. They now understood the source of the behavior, but since it had been learned in the child's home, they did not know how to move across the cultural barriers to talk with his parents about the problem his behavior created for them in the classroom. Such moments led more than one teacher to look forward to the end of the year and declare that the struggle was "about to get me down."

In the past the church school and the circles of the United Methodist Women had been the nerve centers of the congregation. Leadership emerged from the Sunday school classes. Friendly banter about comparative attendance and classroom teaching styles underscored

a sense of vitality and strength. Adult classes sponsored congregational events and often raised extra funds to cover unbudgeted and
unexpected expenses in the church. Poor pastoral leadership at points
over the years, we were told, had contributed to the shift of some
authority for the working of the church to the leadership of the Sunday school. With strong and creative pastoral leadership and with
growing numbers of people experiencing worship as the primary
agency in forming the vision and values of congregational life, the
role of the Sunday school as a primary center for teaching and learning in the congregation had become less clear.

CONGREGATIONAL CURRICULUM

The interplay of explicit, implicit, and null curricular themes in
the life of the Northwoods church is more turbulent than in Cedar
Grove or Oakhurst. Old themes co-exist with new. At times they
contradict, reinforce, and alter one another. Occasionally the encounter of old and new creates something quite unexpected. The
tenuous and evolving character of congregational life is perhaps
most evident in the efforts of long-time members simultaneously
to face down the death of long-held notions of church while, at
the same time, to create a new kind of church. At the same time
many newer members seek a fellowship of affirmation and acceptance to help them survive in an alien land. Out of the mix of these
ways of entering into and being church several themes have begun
to emerge, giving shape and direction to the way the people of
Northwoods understand themselves to be church. These themes
provide clues to an emerging congregational curriculum for teaching and learning.[5]

A Sign of the Cross: Faith of Loss

The Northwoods community and the Northwoods Church have
changed significantly since the new sanctuary was completed in 1972.
They continue to experience change. Change can mean opportunity,
and that has been our focus up to this point. With change, however,
also comes loss, and the experience of many losses haunts many
long-time members. Friends have moved away. Others have transferred to other churches. Some return to visit, but most of these relationships have been lost. The inevitability that others will also move
and that others will die only heightens the sense of loss.

Another experience of loss occurred around the diminishing power of community and church organizations and traditions to engage and mobilize people. Efforts to revive the old neighborhood association received considerable publicity in the city newspapers, especially for the emphasis on advantages of a culturally diverse neighborhood, but they could not be sustained. When some Vietnamese residents in the neighborhood cut down the trees that had given the subdivision its name in order to provide more sun for their gardens, the sense of loss among long-time residents escalated into a clash of values. The expansion of Asian and Hispanic businesses and the creation of small shopping malls catering to specific ethnic markets altered the character of neighborhood shopping. Many nearby shops no longer attract long-time residents; instead, they draw people from all over the metropolitan area. Thus they no longer serve as places for common gathering and conversation.

The sense of loss can be heard as some of the long-time members describe the family-centered activities of the church when their own children were young or the importance of the now closed elementary school to the sense of community among neighborhood residents. It can be heard in words that hint at a sense of burnout among some of the long-time members when they talk about their struggle to keep the church going when membership and financial resources plummeted. It is evident in the complaints and negative comments among a few remaining members of the church who do not approve or appreciate the decision of the Administrative Council to become a multicultural congregation.

The sense of loss can be discerned in little ways as well. It becomes evident when long-time residents long for the ability to say more than "hello" to non–English-speaking neighbors or strain to understand the words of another church member reading one of the weekly scripture lessons with an unfamiliar accent; in the struggles of the board of trustees seeking ways to secure the building after a series of break-ins; in the struggles of the finance committee or Administrative Council to think creatively about ways to meet the budget; or when individuals realize they lack the moral support of their neighbors to help stop destructive behavior on the part of outsiders who happen into the community.

The sense of loss does not belong only to those who have been a part of the Northwoods community for some time. New members know the loss of family, friends, and communities just as profoundly. Members from Liberia suffer the loss of their homeland. They live with the realization they cannot go home—at least until the political climate changes. They cannot see members of their families and other loved ones who remain. For many the cost of leaving has been high. Their educational experience has not been honored in this new country. Their financial well-being has been severely curtailed. The familiarity of language, custom, and tradition is gone. Their experience of loss is very tangible and specific. Ethnic and national identity, especially for youth of African heritage, is confused by the racial history of this nation.

Robert Bellah, a prominent sociologist of religion, coined the phrase "faith of loss" to describe the ability, even the willingness, to accept, duly mourn, and then move on faithfully into whatever new situation or challenge an individual or group faces.[6] This acknowledgment of the need to move on despite the sense of profound loss can be heard frequently in the conversations and actions of long-time and new members. It occurred most clearly in the decisions of the Administrative Council to work toward becoming a congregation embracing cultural diversity, to bring a Hispanic couple on staff, and to try bilingual worship services. It occurs almost everyday as long-time members fend off the words of friends who say the quest to be culturally diverse is futile. It is heard in the words of people transplanted from other parts of the world as they claim the church to be "their home." The decision to accept responsibility to help create this new community becomes an act of faith. So do the bonds of friendship linking people with radically different cultural heritages. In moments like these, faith in the future triumphs over the pain of loss. It creates in church members, however, an experience of liminality or of living between rather than in the center of cultural and social relationships).[7]

Two issues heighten this sense of liminality integral to a faith of loss in this congregation. The first is race. This issue has rarely been overt. Some attribute the lack of controversy over the growing presence of black persons in the congregation to the civility and genuine care for others people experience in Winston and his wife. As people recently from Africa or the Caribbean joined the congregation, members of the church encountered a similar lack of tension over issues of race. Some members of Northwoods did have and continue to have difficulty with the presence of persons whose skin color is different from their own. But the traditional patterns of black-and-white relationships in the southern United States have not dominated congregational interaction.

On several occasions when the subject has surfaced in a committee meeting, Winston carefully described how in his own experience he does not see people as black or white. Those distinctions, while obvious to the eye, have little bearing on the character of the relationships of the people he knew while growing up in Barbados or while pastoring congregations in the Caribbean with black and white members from several nations. He cannot recall race being an issue in these predominantly black societies. But race *is* an issue in the United States.

The dynamics of race are felt in a variety of ways in this church— some positive and some negative. No one acted surprised or upset, from what we could tell, when a European-American boy and Liberian girl sat together during the worship service and could occasionally be seen holding hands. One of the European-American boys transferred to another school because he felt oppressed as a minority student. He and one of the Liberian boys seemed to have some running disagreement which broke out on at least one occasion into a fight during Sunday school. When in the "safety" of old friends, a few European-American adults in the congregation will talk about their feeling that blacks are taking over the city. One of the Liberian teen-agers writes poetry to focus his quest to understand what it means to be African and black in the United States. This undercurrent is confronted, as Jerome pointed out on more than one occasion, when the congregation gathers around the communion table to receive in first a black hand, then a white hand, then a brown hand, the gifts of God's grace.

The dynamics of liminality probably have been experienced by congregational members around issues of language more than race. Despite inspirational moments, such as when a Mexican-American woman sang "How Great Thou Art" in Spanish or when a trio of women sang "O For a Thousand Tongues" in English, Spanish, and Mano, the task of communicating among people who do not understand each other has been daunting. When the language is complicated by differences in socioeconomic class and cultural assumptions about the roles of men and women, tensions often have become real. English-speaking Sunday school teachers who struggled to communicate with children who could not understand them left their classrooms exhausted. Printed bulletins during bilingual services of worship frustrated Spanish-speaking members whose Roman Catholic and Pentecostal backgrounds had not prepared them to follow church bulletins and hymns sung from books. Some women struggled with the macho patterns of relating they experienced in the Spanish-speaking male lay pastor. Some of the older Liberian women found the familiarity of American U.S. children disrespectful. Linguistic and cultural differences, in other words, created gaps that could only be bridged by appreciating the reality of the differences involved.

A Sign of Possibility: Gathering Up the Tribes and Nations

Repeatedly through the year, in sermons, through his teaching, and in the church newsletter, Jerome continued to explore the possibilities of being a church fashioned in the multicultural image of Revelation 7, in which "all tribes, tongues, and nations" gather to praise God. No one in the congregation knew how to go about living into that new vision. Certainly the pastors did not. Jerome reminded folks that he was "just a country boy from southern Alabama, in itself a distinctive cultural group." But this ignorance did not seem to prevent people from trying.

Often the processional on Sunday morning dynamically illustrated the act of gathering up people from many nations: teen-agers with Liberian, Mexican, and European heritages leading the processional; women from Panama, Liberia, and Jamaica in the choir; pastors from Alabama and Barbados following behind.

Winston may have illustrated the dynamic of gathering people from all over the world into the act of worship most clearly during one of his conversations with children. He had just returned from a trip to Asia, where he attended a meeting of the World Methodist Evangelism Institute of the World Methodist Council. Gathering the children around him at the foot of the communion table, he showed the children a picture of a painting by Norman Rockwell depicting people from all over the globe. He pointed to one face in the picture and said he had met a person from the same country. Then he pointed to a member of the congregation and said that he or she had also come from that country. He pointed to another picture and introduced the children to another person in the congregation. "We are connected as God's children," he concluded, "to people all over the world."

The Northwoods church building and the care people give it enhance the possibilities in the image of "gathering the tribes and nations" as a viable alternative perspective on congregational identity and mission. Jerome made this clear during a sermon illustrating how the building of the sanctuary helped prepare the way for the congregation to embrace a changing constituency. The architecture, Jerome observed, declared that God was at the center of the community, which formed around the symbols of the presence of God. In Northwoods, however, the architect made sure that one cannot look upon that center without seeing the faces of others across the room. When people are gathered to worship in the Northwoods church building, they see the world, at least symbolically, engaged in the common task of worshiping the Creator of all peoples. Without anyone realizing it at the time, the architect helped prepare the way for a new kind of church community. This new community, Jerome has suggested in several sermons, only reveals a vision of the church long submerged in the depths of the Christian subconscious. When the Northwoods congregation gathers in that octagon building around the cross and table, it has the potential of living into the promise in that vision.

In Luke 14 Jesus tells a parable about a man who prepared a great dinner party, but none of the guests he invited consented to come. So he sent his servants "into the streets and byways" to gather in anyone they could find to fill the house and to enjoy the feast. The Northwoods congregation is a little like the man in the parable: A great feast is being prepared on that table, which centers their lives. The building has been well-maintained despite diminishing financial resources by teams of men and women under the leadership and labor of the board of trustees and many of the women from the United Methodist Women. Flowers on the table have been carefully arranged. The choir stretches the boundaries of its members' musical experience to teach and lead the congregation in music from around the world. The liturgy balances order and form with warmth and spontaneity.

Saddened but undaunted by changing demographics of church and community, people who have chosen to stay at Northwoods carefully prepare the table as if for a party. Jerome had declared they should gather all (or consciously seek to recruit anyone who would come) from within a three-mile radius of the church. Door-to-door surveys were conducted with teams of adults and teen-agers. The youth organized an event to invite Vietnamese residents in the neighborhood to the church. Even though no Vietnamese showed up, it became an opportunity to learn more about that nation and its culture. A Spanish language service was instituted so those who did not speak English would have a place at the table. Multilingual worship services were designed to bring everyone together in a common act of praise and thanksgiving.

During the 1991-92 winter months Jerome preached a sermon around anthropologist Edward T. Hall's observation that different groups of people move to different rhythmic beats. In one of his books Hall describes a research project that involved filming school children at play. When slowed down to the point that the researchers could observe the movements of the children's feet, hands, and bodies, they discerned a clear pattern to their movements—a kind of dance with a beat strong enough to include all the children on the playground. Much of Hall's research has been directed to the exploration of these distinctive rhythmic patterns—the beat—in several different cultures and how they govern the ways people interact and relate to each other. Persons who enter a group with an unfamiliar beat will not know how to interact and relate appropriately.[8]

Jerome realized that in a diverse community, people need to learn the beat in the lives of others in order to communicate and get along. Thus he has placed an increased emphasis on listening for "the heartbeat of God" in order to stay in rhythm with the Divine, attending to the diversity of rhythms and beats within the congregation in order to enhance communication with each other, and discerning the beat(s) in the community around the church in order to reach out and interact appropriately with their neighbors. This conscious attention to "the beat" has become an important theme for Northwoods. It appears in bold letters on the weekly newsletter, seeps into congregational conversation as the choir director teaches a new hymn with a rhythm unfamiliar to many, and permeates Jerome's reflections on the congregation's common life. The beat creates a theoretical structure for gathering the congregation into ministry through *Upreach*—the committee concerned with the relationship of the congregation to God; *Inreach*—the committee concerned with the spiritual and social development of congregational life; and *Outreach*—the committee responsible for the congregation's ministries in the neighborhood and beyond. Even the names convey a pattern of movement.

The task of discerning the growing variety of rhythmic patterns in the congregation has not been easy. Perhaps the most obvious example centers around when people gather. Several different understandings of the meaning of time shape the responses of peoples from different groups to any event. The gathering for Sunday morning worship usually begins about 10:25 A.M. with announcements and the sharing of congregational concerns. The prelude usually begins around 10:30 A.M. or whenever the announcements are concluded. Some Liberian members *arrive for church* at 11:00 A.M. For some Spanish-speaking members an event is only *getting started* when European-American members are preparing to go home. Jerome has begun to talk about these differences when making announcements of special events in the life of the church. But differences around the meaning of time, for the most part, frustrate almost everyone.

Perhaps the most painful experience for Northwoods over the different rhythmic patterns among its members occurred on Christmas Eve. Expectations were quite high for this event—a popular one among long-time members and one that took place after a successful concert of Hispanic religious music involving groups from several Spanish-speaking congregations. The planning for Christmas Eve started late in the season and it followed the traditional process of the Upreach committee. Elements in the liturgy were identified and roles assigned to people from both Spanish- and English-speaking congregations. It proved to be a painful experience for all participants. The leadership appeared awkward and ill at ease. Parts of the service involved translation and other parts did not. This confused people. Some of the music was unfamiliar and was introduced without explanation. Expectations were not met and negative evaluations of the event by the staff and Administrative Council were candid and to the point. Some wondered whether the church could ever do a bilingual service.

The pain of that event, however, led to the decision that the next bilingual service would involve a culturally diverse planning committee, whose work would be complete in time for unfamiliar parts of the service to be practiced in Sunday school classes, choir rehearsals, and prior to the worship service itself. Those involved in the leadership would also practice their parts so that "the beat" might gather up the "beats" in the congregation. The outcome of that decision was the Pentecost Sunday service in June.

A committee representing the cultural diversity of the congregation planned the service over several weeks. Extensive rehearsals in the choir and Sunday school classes as well as with both congregations prior to worship contributed to an atmosphere of anticipation and confidence among the more than fifty people who provided leadership in some way during the service. On this occasion the multiplicity of "beats" seemed right. When the service ended, most people asked that other worship events in the future be more like this one. Eight people, however, also decided they could not handle so much strangeness and transferred their membership to congregations more like Northwoods used to be. The drama and power of gathering up diverse peoples, in other words, included the pain of separation and loss for some.

A Sign of Trust: Let the Children Lead Them

When Jerome began his ministry in Northwoods, its fragile future was foreshadowed in the empty classrooms and nursery for children. And it has been around the growing numbers of children and youth that some of the most critical learning about what it means to embrace cultural diversity as an integral part of the Northwoods' identity has occurred. Nowhere has the change in the cultural composition of the congregation been more visible. Cultural heritages among the youth include Liberian, Mexican, Thai, Canadian, and Caribbean, as well as African American and European American. The backgrounds of the children are even more varied.

When Winston and Jerome came to Northwoods in 1990, one Sunday school class encompassing all ages took in the few children in the church and one class served all the youth. No nursery was needed. When the children's ministries coordinator began plans for the fall Sunday school schedule for 1992, four classes plus an infant/toddler nursery were required for all the children who were coming.

Once again, children and youth are giving shape to congregational life. Like a doting but strict grandmother, one of the older women in the congregation oversees the older children, youth, and young adults who serve as acolytes. As they lead the choir and staff into worship, these young people with Hispanic, African, Asian, and European backgrounds project a culturally diverse image for the congregation's future. Older children and youth take their turns with the rest of the laity of the church in reading the scripture lessons each Sunday morning. Winston gathers as many as twenty black, white, and brown children around him for the children's sermon and often employs senior high youth in the telling of a story. This time together not only serves to instruct the young, but it reminds adults in the congregation of their culturally diverse identity and mission. The youth, who as a group claim they cannot sing, are always willing to create a dramatic presentation for worship or fellowship dinners with the help of their Sunday school teacher. The two children's choirs, which sing on occasion in worship, are just as likely to be included in a musical number with the adult choir as they are to sing alone. When Jerome concludes the worship service by urging members to "greet your neighbor with a handshake, hug, or kiss," several adults take time to greet children, and many youth seek out adult friends. One long-time adult member of the congregation reported that a spontaneous hug from a child who could not speak English convinced him of the value of a multilingual ministry.

Winston Worrell has done much to foster intergenerational relations at Northwoods. Besides focusing the attention on the young people in his children's sermons most Sundays, he supports the Sunday school teachers and youth counselors in a quiet and consistent manner. He involves the youth in activities often left to those much older. They participate in the neighborhood visitation program, meeting in the homes of older members of the congregation and visiting older members recuperating from major illness or surgery. Their youth retreats and involvement in judicatory activities reinforce the ties that bind this very culturally diverse group of young people. Indeed, most sit together to the right of the choir loft and pulpit on Sunday mornings, illustrating on a weekly basis that youth from diverse cultural backgrounds can overcome cultural barriers to create a close-knit fellowship.

But the high visibility of youth has also been nurtured by several lay persons who continued to advocate for youth in the church even during the days when few youth could be found. Perhaps the relationship between a number of the youth and the adults of the congregation is best illustrated by recounting an event that occurred during the 1993 Maundy Thursday service. This service in the congregation included the reenactment of the washing of the feet of the disciples by Jesus. Small towels were available for people in the congregation to pick up as they asked others if they might symbolically wash their feet. After the youth had wiped the shoes of one another, a Mexican-American teen-ager tentatively approached the older European-American woman who guided the acolyte program of which he was a part. He stooped to wipe her shoes. As he stood back up, she gave him a big spontaneous hug. His action prompted the rest of the youth (black, white, and brown) to move through the congregation to initiate the act of wiping the feet of their elders. This liturgical action intensified the identification of many in the congregation with the sacrificial ministry of Jesus. It also dramatized the binding of generations in the congregation across racial and ethnic lines. For many, it also revealed something of what it might mean to be a *multicultural* congregation.

SUMMARY

The journey into discovering what it means to be a community of faith that embraces cultural diversity has just begun for the Northwoods congregation. With a leap of faith over the despair of a rapidly declining membership and a growing spiritual malaise, its leaders found hope for their own future in their new pastor's re-articulation of a New Testament image of church encompassing the peoples of the world. A commitment to reaching out to others through mission, a vital liturgical tradition, strong fellowship groups in the adult Sunday school, effective pastoral leadership, and a building that conveys hospitality to those who visit provide impetus to the transformation of congregational identity that this decision demands.

As we completed our study, the membership of the church re-flected significant progress toward the fulfillment of that vision. More than twelve nations were represented among those who gather regu-larly for worship. The first African Americans had joined. Despite decisions to focus attention on a Spanish-speaking ministry, by far the largest group of new members was originally from Liberia. The bonds between some old and some new members had reached the point that negotiations over expectations and procedures in congre-gational life have become more complicated. The stories of the Ce-dar Grove and Oakhurst churches would suggest that the Northwoods folk are about to embark on another phase of the jour-ney—the development of new power dynamics for making the deci-sions that will give shape to congregational life and mission in the future. This next step is causing some apprehension, but for both long-time and new members the experience of holding hands around the communion table while praying the Lord's Prayer keeps before them the image of what it might mean to be a multicultural church.

Notes

1. Northwoods was the first congregation in the region to adopt this architectural style. It has since been copied and adapted by many other churches.

2. The *Atlanta Journal/The Atlanta Constitution* (December 13, 1993), B:1.

3. A member of the committee at the time theorized the closing of the church would not have been a problem for the Annual Conference. People could transfer to other United Methodist churches nearby (the closest only three miles away). The building could be sold without encumbering the Conference, since the debt had nearly been eliminated.

4. Members of the church apparently had little awareness of the com-plex ideological issues surrounding their image of a multicultural congrega-tion. They implied in their own usage that the church would have a membership drawn from diverse cultural heritages (see chapter 1, page 30, for a discussion of the variety of ways this term has been used).

5. The task of naming the themes in the curriculum of Northwoods contrasted with that for Cedar Grove and Oakhurst. In those two churches the language for the signs evoking the themes belonged to the people of the churches. The congregational vocabulary at Northwoods, however, proved to be much more fluid. Therefore, we found ourselves drawing on our own experience for language to give order and meaning to what we heard and experienced.

6. Robert N. Bellah, *Beyond Belief: Essays on Religion in a Post-Traditional World* (New York: Harper & Row, 1970), xix and passim—"faith in spite of the brokenness of every human structure . . . "

7. "The attributes of liminality of liminal personae ('threshold people') are necessarily ambiguous, since this condition and these persons elude or slip through the network of classifications that normally locate states and positions in cultural space. Liminal entities are neither here nor there; they are betwixt and between the positions assigned and arrayed by law, custom, convention, and ceremonial. . . . [These threshold people] tend to develop an intense comradeship and egalitarianism. Secular distinctions of rank and status disappear or are homogenized" (Victor Turner, *Ritual Process: Structure and Anti-Structure* [Ithaca, NY: Cornell Paperbacks, 1991 {1997}], 95).

8. Edward T. Hall, *The Dance of Life: The Other Dimension of Time* (Garden City, NY: Anchor Press/Doubleday, 1983).

5

VOLUNTARY DIVERSITY

An Emerging Ecclesiology

"This church works because they're here [the whites who took a stand and stayed], Rev. Martha's here, and we're here [the newer black members]."

—High school teacher and coach

Worldly differences fail to separate our folk. Instead, these differences are the threads that the love of Jesus Christ weaves into the one tapestry—Oakhurst Presbyterian Church.

—Mission Statement

INTRODUCTION

Many clues point to the denominational affiliations of Cedar Grove, Oakhurst, and Northwoods churches. Each displays its denominational name in prominent letters on the signboard outside the church building and on all printed materials. They use denominational hymnals in worship. Committees are organized according to denominational guidelines, although Northwoods has developed its own nomenclature for them. Pastoral placements follow denominational procedures. Denominational mission priorities and programs are supported. Cedar Grove and Northwoods, according to the Methodist custom, request forgiveness of their "trespasses" when reciting the Lord's Prayer and gather at the communion rail for the Eucharist. In contrast, Oakhurst confesses its "debts" in the same prayer and partakes of the eucharistic elements in unison while seated in the pews according to Presbyterian custom. Members of Oakhurst reveal their reformation heritage in discussions of their covenantal relationship with God, while members of the two United Methodist congregations draw attention to their Wesleyan tradition when they refer to their common life as a sign of God's grace.

At the same time, Cedar Grove, Oakhurst, and Northwoods churches are not like most Presbyterian and United Methodist congregations. This difference becomes most clear in the unambiguous affirmation of the contribution of racial and cultural diversity to their identity and mission. That explicit affirmation sets the frame for embracing other differences—most visibly socioeconomic class and sexual orientation at Oakhurst, linguistic differences at Northwoods,[1] and intergenerational differences in all three congregations. Although the embrace of diversity challenges the faith and practices of church members, these differences have come to be viewed not so much as problems to be overcome but as gifts to be accepted, explored, and affirmed.

When a congregation's identity is distinguished, in part, by its embrace of the diversity in the human community, it challenges the emphasis upon cultural homogeneity and like-mindedness operative in most United States congregations. In the pages that follow, we will explore several ways in which cultural diversity influences how these congregations view themselves to be church.

EMBRACING DIFFERENCES

Northwoods describes its church building as a place where "the world gathers to worship"—a world of people at its doorstep from many cultures and with many languages, diverse customs, and traditions. Cedar Grove welcomes into its family whoever happens to be present. Oakhurst's mission statement makes explicit the range of differences central to its identity as a community of faith. Its members "come from many different places, many different economic levels, from different countries of the world." Its members are "young and old, black and white, male and female, employed and unemployed, poor and comfortable, strong and broken, courageous and disheartened, able and sick, hurt and healers." Other differences could be added: heterosexual and homosexual, musical and non-musical, highly educated and unschooled, ordained and lay, conservative and liberal. The world, they contend, "uses these [and other] categories to separate people from one another." At Oakhurst these differences find their "beauty and strength" in the ecclesial activity of weaving their lives together into the "Oakhurst tapestry."

The decision to embrace difference has been made official in each congregation through the actions of their administrative committees and mission statements. But the decision to embrace the differences these congregations experience must be renewed whenever an encounter disturbs the familiar or whenever the familiar becomes suddenly strange. For new folks, the decision to embrace difference occurs when they begin to contemplate the possibility of becoming members. Some put that decision off, even while attending regularly, due to strong ties to another congregation or denomination. Others wonder, often with some apprehension, if the acceptance they experience will continue indefinitely. Can they trust those "others" whom they have been taught for much of their lives to view with some wariness? For others, especially at Oakhurst, the embrace of difference is linked to a radical commitment to social justice. Men especially struggle with the challenge this commitment places on them. For European-American men the difficulty arises from the explicit identification of the plight of African-American men with the domination of white men. For African-American men the prophetic articulation of the social and economic situation of black men in U.S. society by a white male pastor requires them to respond to a *black* message delivered by a *white* pastoral leader. For both groups this encounter with difference is confrontational and unsettling. The challenge, although more subtle, is no less demanding in the other two churches. The decision to embrace the diversity in these congregations requires every person to consider suspending many perspectives and practices that perpetuate social hierarchies and enclaves based on categories especially of race and culture, but also of gender and generation.

The decision to join any of these congregations involves a corresponding decision *not* to join a congregation that enjoys a much higher degree of cultural homogeneity and a more recognizable pattern of social organization. An African American dramatized this point as he recalled his ambivalence about joining Cedar Grove— "It was awful white." The decision to become part of a predominantly European-American congregation (with a white female pastor, at the time) meant he was also deciding against driving back to the African-American church he and his family had belonged to for many years; against a traditionally black style of worship; and against gendered patterns of black church pastoral authority and lay responsivity. He also had to live with charges from others in the African-American community that he and his family were "selling out."

Recurrent encounters with difference similarly heighten feelings of ambivalence about staying in the congregation. A European-American woman whose membership at Northwoods spans more than three decades discovered, for example, that when the vision of a church made up of peoples from many nations caught her imagination, she not only found herself rejecting the image of church she had helped develop over many years, but she was herself rejected by many of her long-time friends who ridiculed the new direction of the congregation. Some of her friends chose to leave in search of a more familiar church setting. She chose to develop new friends and remain.

Little things often trigger experiences of ambivalence about the extent to which one can live into a consciousness of the dynamics of difference. Some Northwoods members, for example, found the singing of The Lord's Prayer to a popular Caribbean tune with a calypso beat almost sacrilegious, even revolting. Caribbean members who heard this reaction felt deep pain. Many African Americans in all three congregations grow weary of what some among them call the "lack of rhythm and beat" when they sing traditional European hymns. A commitment to embrace difference in all three churches, however, means confronting something new and unexpected in each other as an ever-present possibility. At times members tire of this expanding consciousness of the dynamics of difference. But, for the most part, the embrace of difference energizes their participation and intensifies their sense of wonder over the many ways in which God might be working through them.

In the embrace of difference these congregations and others like them throughout the country stand over against the dominant traditions of voluntary church life in the United States. They challenge the commitment to homogeneity dominating ministry strategies in Protestant churches. The pervasiveness of this commitment to homogeneity, for example, undergirds Peter Wagner's theological rationale for evangelism church growth strategies. Although Wagner affirmed the value of the witness of culturally diverse congregations like the three in this study, his prior and deeper commitment to the Great Commission to evangelize the world (or to bring all peoples into the church) also led him to conclude that "God is pleased with

Christian congregations that gather together people who come mainly from one homogeneous unit." For Wagner, the prior concern of the church should be the salvation of *all* individuals rather than the character and witness of the membership of any given congregation or its mission. Affirming the notion that people prefer to associate "with their own kind," Wagner contends that "disciples are more readily made by people within their own homogeneous unit, and congregations develop into healthy communities when they concentrate on only one kind of people." He concludes that this "innate sense of (racially and culturally homogenous) community should be seen in a positive light" and that people should not feel obligated to mix people across cultural differences when forming or strengthening congregations.[2]

Members in each of these congregations recognize the appeal of Wagner's statement, but vehemently disagree. Despite the necessity of repeatedly choosing to embrace difference, they see in their own experience an alternative possibility for ecclesial life. Their pastors locate that alternative in biblical and theological traditions often hidden from view by dominant cultural ideologies. The family rhetoric of Cedar Grove gives concrete expression, for example, to Letty Russell's vision of an ecclesia in which its congregation's members are *partners* before they "know one another, because God has reached out to us in Jesus Christ and has reconciled us, making us partners of one another and God." This *partnership* leads church members into "a pattern of equal regard and mutual acceptance" in Cedar Grove's case, between African American and European American, and among children, youth, and adults.[3] Each week when the Northwoods congregation gathers for worship, it illustrates the shift from an ecclesial image of church as "a household ruled by a patriarch to one of a household where everyone gathers around the common table to break bread and to share table talk and hospitality."[4] In the sharing of congregational concerns at Oakhurst, as in the radical egalitarianism Elizabeth Schüssler Fiorenza discerns in the early manifestations of the church, everyone who wishes to speak (and therefore, in the congregation's mission, also to serve) has the freedom to do so.[5] Many members of these congregations would affirm Sharon Welch's observation that the "aims of equality and respect are met" most clearly in highlighting their differences rather than in "some common foundation" to give coherence to their sense of being church together.[6] This does not mean a diminished christology in their theological commitments. Instead, the focus of their faith commitment tends to emphasize the reality of Christ as the sacramental incarnation of

God—the one with us, who comes as brother, and as justice, peace, and hope.

Perhaps because the embrace of difference so deeply challenges the bias to homogeneity in voluntary church life for Protestant U.S. Americans, it does not come easily or quickly. Cedar Grove's story illustrates something of the movement involved in the shift from ecclesial homogeneity to ecclesial heterogeneity experienced in each congregation. When faced with a dwindling membership, Cedar Grove reached a crisis point. In order to survive, church leaders decided to be an inclusive church—"Whosoever will come, let them come" became their motto. Inclusivity, they discovered in retrospect, is not the same as the celebration of difference. Church members thought they had opened their doors to the "others" moving into their community, but almost no one accepted their invitation. Cedar Grove's policy of inclusion was premised on the prominent ideology of the period, that of basic similarity—"It doesn't matter what the color of your skin, we're all the same underneath." In other words, the European-American members of the church believed they could afford to let African Americans in because "they are really the same as us" underneath—they will be assimilated into our church and into our identity. Cedar Grove members may have begun to move beyond a color barrier to a sense of the mutual regard and acceptance Russell identifies as characteristic of ecclesia, but they had not yet accepted the relationship of color to culture radically affecting social relationships in the United States. A similar step toward becoming a culturally diverse congregation also occurred at Northwoods. Some members, at least, now acknowledge that they initially embraced a vision of the church as a fellowship of persons from many nations to facilitate their assimilation into the dominant U.S. American and Christian culture.

With the leadership of Rev. Martha, Cedar Grove began to chip away at its ideology of inclusiveness with increasingly egalitarian patterns of relationship. By 1990 the congregation's membership had become more than 50 percent African American. The remaining European Americans continued to be committed to the life of their church, no matter who might come. White and black members held equitable positions of leadership in the church and the community. The church now *belonged* to its African-American members as well as to its European-American members.[7] The surprise to both was the extent to which cultural differences persisted in shaping their common life. African-American members had not been assimilated into the church as much as the church had adjusted to reflect their presence in it. And the white folk continued to struggle (with an increasing sense of hope for their future) to adjust to this new reality. Worship style and music had changed (despite the continuing leadership of a European-American pastor and choir director); fellowship suppers and other social events were noticeably different. The church was now recognizably black to some extent and recognizably white to some extent,[8] with negotiation constantly being necessary whenever cultural preferences or views on how things ought to be differed. Schüssler Fiorenza might call the emerging ecclesiology through these negotiations, "a community of equality."[9] This involves, as Russell has observed, the recognition that the emerging partnership among groups of people whom society labels as different from each other cannot be defined or planned but is experienced and celebrated as a "gift of God." This gift exists as the "power to love and to be loved," despite the barriers in the world seeking to inhibit such relationships. This emerging sense of mutuality does not "have to do with equality of gifts" among church members or cultural groups.[10] It has more to do with a sense of equality of participation in the gifts of the inexhaustible love of God's Spirit. As Jerome declares each Sunday morning at Northwoods, "God cannot love you more than God does right now." This vision of partnership becomes evident in the declaration at Cedar Grove that "we eat in each other's homes all the time," and at Oakhurst in the persistent, intentional, and collaborative efforts to participate in Christ's breaking down the walls that divide people in the church and community.

Living into a pattern of equal regard and mutual respect, however, presents many challenges to these congregations. Who gets to be an equal? Everyone—children, foreigners, neo-Nazi's, Buddhists? Who gets to be a member? Cedar Grove's openness to the influence of visitors, Oakhurst's recruitment of gays and lesbians, and Northwoods welcoming invitation to a Hindu to join at the Lord's Table challenge common notions of who constitutes membership in most mainline denominations. But the issue goes deeper. Who decides? And how does one adjudicate among competing claims made by equals? That issue tugs at every decision made in all three congregations. When a congregation seeks to embrace diversity, it rejects the notion that any one cultural perspective should establish the criteria for judgments about what is important. It begins to recognize the presence of cultural bias in theological statements, liturgical actions, and organizational structures. Congregational leaders consequently begin to assert the value of a multiplicity of voices and perspectives contributing to the identity and mission of the congregation. This insight leads to a second perspective on what it means to be church emerging from the embrace of difference.

CELEBRATING MULTIPLICITY

The visitor to any of these congregations is bombarded with images and sounds. An encounter with the racial diversity in the membership of each congregation is intensified by dark and light artistic images of Jesus, business suits and Nigerian head tie scarves on worshipers, banners on the walls with symbols drawn from African, Hispanic, and European religious and cultural traditions. Rhythmic patterns in the singing of these congregations range from the somber steady beat of Genevan and Scottish psalters to the praise traditions of African-American and European-American gospel music, to the syncopations of Caribbean and African religious folk music. The narrative structure of the teaching and preaching of each of the pastors engages the cultural experience of church members out of a heightened consciousness of the particularity of their own stories of faith and identity. In their embrace of difference these congregations provide not only a contrasting image of church to that found in more homogeneous congregations, but they illustrate a praxis of multiplicity often described most fully in the postmodern critiques of modernity. These congregations provide an alternative to the dynamics of racial, gender, class, and cultural differences, which establish borders of inclusion and exclusion that, in turn, reproduce models of relationship based on domination, subordination, and inequality.[11]

A commitment to the value of multiplicity influences the ways in which people in these congregations live into a praxis of being church. The celebration of the story of the birth of Christ at Oakhurst described in the third chapter is illustrative in its use of symbols and music and stories traditionally associated with the Sunday school pageant of historic, mainline European-American and African-American U.S. Protestant churches, the African-American celebration of Kwanzaa and the Mexican-American traditions of Poseda. It challenged predilections to cultural exclusivity and cultural superiority in the selection of a cast that included over the years a pregnant African-American teen-ager as Mary, a European-American theological student as Joseph, and women as "wise men." The repetition of the rejection of Mary and Joseph by teen-age innkeepers as the couple moved slowly down the central aisle of the church heightened congregational consciousness to the similar repetition of rejection many in that place had experienced due to racism, sexism, and classism in contemporary institutions. When the script gathered the congregation into singing "We Shall Overcome," this theme song of the Civil Rights Movement seemed a fitting way to proclaim that in Christ the walls of hostility perpetuating patterns of domination and oppression in society have been shattered. In retelling the story of the birth of Christ—in this place, at least—the power of the forces of domination and oppression have been broken. Christ has come, and God's people are free.

The celebration of multiplicity emerges, in part, from the interplay of an examination of the contexts in which these congregations seek to embody the ministry of Jesus Christ and an exploration of the eschatological messages integral to that gospel. Robert Schreiter provides a clue to the first part of this process. Like churches in Latin America, which experienced a significant gap between the theologies they received from Europe and their efforts to talk about their own experience theologically, these three congregations persistently find themselves faced with a gap between the theological questions they ask and the traditional answers given to those questions in their ecclesial traditions. In the pageant of Christ's birth the Oakhurst context distinctively shapes the telling of the story. The mother of Jesus becomes, for example, an unmarried and pregnant teen-ager. Themes of homelessness, poverty, oppression, and injustice run through the script.

No one could miss the juxtaposition of the glory surrounding the church's celebration of the incarnation and the reality of life as lived by people in the time of Joseph and Mary and today. The drama of music, light, and movement identified with hymns and scripture texts deeply rooted in the collective memories of church members conveys messages of wonder and awe. Reminders of the disparities of rich and poor, powerful and powerless locate that ancient story in the midst of contemporary practices of injustice and oppression. In this contextualization of one of the most familiar events in the church year, Oakhurst (and in similar fashion, Cedar Grove and Northwoods) seeks to create a "new kind of Christian identity," one that grows specifically out of the engagement of the local context with gospel traditions. Schreiter has called such efforts "local theologies."[12]

The process of doing local theology engages people in the dialectical interaction of gospel, church, and culture. In the movement back and forth among these three texts, members ask questions about congregational life, its relationship to the traditions of faith, the response of the congregation to the experience of people in that social setting, and the congregation's approach to social change—all guided, Schreiter emphasizes, "by the presence of the Spirit within the community." These questions become the impetus to local theological reflection and to local ministry practices. The shape of the common life of a congregation, in turn, grows out of the ordering of its corporate responses to these questions.[13]

The examination of the context of gospel, church, and, in the case of these congregations, several cultures, takes as many forms as there are congregations or communities of faith. Rev. Martha, for example, makes a daily circuit of the shops and schools throughout the Cedar Grove community to "take its pulse." Jerome listens attentively to some church members describe being forced to leave their country—losing, in the process, contact with family members, economic well-being, social status, and the comfort of being in a familiar cultural setting. As he listens he discerns new theological meanings from the efforts of his own southern Alabama sharecropper family to eke out a living during the Depression years. Nibs insists that everyone who has a concern to share should have the full freedom to speak or sing it in worship services and other church gatherings. As they do so they illustrate the extent and depth of the struggle and pain found in the negotiations of the members of that congregation with illness, death, discrimination, excessive expectations, and the joy they occasionally experience when those burdens are lifted.

The examination of context leads to changes in congregational perceptions and practices. When Oakhurst Church gathers to celebrate the story of the birth of Jesus, it calls on those traditionally on the margins of the church and larger community to give witness to the meaning and power of that story. When Northwoods gathers around the table to pray for the church, community, city, nations of origin of church members, and the world, the specific burdens and joys of church members become the shared petitions of the whole community. When Cedar Grove identifies an issue in the community as the focus of some ministry response, the commitment to the transformation of the dehumanizing elements in their contexts becomes evident. The celebration of multiplicity, in other words, begins with a movement to examine the context of each congregation—in both its local and global manifestations—as the impetus to respond to the ministry of Jesus Christ to reconcile and to make whole all of creation. It involves a recognition that every theology and every congregational practice is "a construction of particular persons and faith communities who confess their faith in God in a language, meta-

phor, and thought pattern appropriate to that context."[14] Any theological construction or ministry practice is consequently dependent
on the "standpoint" or contextual location of the people involved.

The other dynamic in the praxis of celebrating multiplicity shifts
the authority for their ministries from what might be called memories of the past to memories of the future in the past. We did not find
ready explanations for the eschatalogical emphasis in the ways these
congregations and their pastors relate scripture to the traditions of
Christian faith and to the contexts of daily living. Perhaps a clue
may be found in their realization that relying upon authorities rooted
in the past has not served many of the people in these congregations
or the churches themselves very well. Certainly the European-American bias in the theological traditions of the denominations of the
three congregations posed problems for many African Americans.
A number of women, especially at Oakhurst, stumbled over the
patriarchal and hierarchical assumptions in those same traditions.
For the Liberians of Northwoods, the past was filled with a great
sense of loss. They could only look back on the political, economic,
and religious shambles of the country they had fled with a longing
not unlike that of the Jews in Babylon. Each of the churches had a
heyday that could no longer inspire the collective imaginations of
their present constituencies for a new future. Each of the congregations had ambivalent feelings about the interventions of denominational leaders. Institutional and, especially at this point of their
common life, theological authorities from the past did not inspire
much promise.

Instead, eschatological visions grounded in the Jewish and Christian memories of the future have become the impetus to the identity
and vocation of these congregations. Our repetition in these chapters of their primary images—nations and tribes gathered around
the throne of the lamb, Christ's shattering of the walls of hostility, or
of family gathered around the banquet table of a host whose graciousness exceeds our human imaginations—parallels their frequent
repetition by pastors and lay leaders whenever they try to explain
who they are as church. Many view their efforts in creating a community that embraces differences as participating in the creative edge
of God's work in the world. The pastors reinforce this view as they
lead people in the exploration of possibilities for their common life
in the visions for the future deeply rooted in the collective memory
of Christian communities. This process has created a sense of openness to new possibility for their identities and mission. They engage
in program planning less to predict or control the consequences of

their efforts than to anticipate new experiences and insights. They see themselves on some uncharted road participating in God's creative and liberative activity.

Letty Russell has called this approach to eschatology "adventology in which God's New Creation is coming into our lives now, bringing the dimension of the holy into the everyday dynamics of human interaction and expectancy."[15] In this effort no one seeks to "get all persons to accept one neat priority system for theological truth but, rather, welcomes all who are willing to share in building a community of human wholeness that is inclusive of women and men of every race and class." These congregations would add children and youth to Russell's vision of an authority rooted in the partnership of community.[16]

The eschatological praxis in celebrating multiplicity focused the script for Oakhurst's Christmas pageant on the possibility of incarnation in the present. It made Cedar Grove's decision to build a gym as a way to reach out to the people of the community seem possible. One of the most powerful examples occurred at Northwoods shortly after the completion of the formal part of this study. After consulting with several members of the church about what to do after the Spanish-speaking ministry pulled out of the church following a moving multilingual and multicultural Pentecost worship service, the chair of the Administrative Council and Jerome invited all the elected officers of the church and anyone else who might want to participate to a "Prayer Meeting for Discernment," seeking God's will for their future. A large group showed up. Pain and grief were prevailing moods. The circle filled the fellowship hall. The meeting began with prayer. Jerome outlined the sequence of events leading up to the departure of the Spanish-speaking ministry. He then invited people to listen to a series of biblical passages and questions, each followed by about ten minutes of silent prayer and another fifteen minutes and more of sharing what people had heard through their quiet reflections. Phrased in colloquial language, the questions prompted responses ranging from feelings to descriptions of experience to theological affirmations.[17] They included words of confession, thanksgiving, joyful remembrance, frustration, hope. By the end of the session the consensus was clear. The Spanish-speaking ministry had not failed. It had been a powerful gift to the congregation. It had brought joy as well as pain. People had become more aware of what is required in the embrace of diversity. The church would remain open to God's leading in whatever new direction their commitment to being a multicultural congregation might take them.

Although the form differed from Oakhurst's Christmas pageant, this prayer meeting shared a common function. The people of Northwoods had gathered into a process of local theological reflection. One participant summed up the group's discernment of God's will:

> To be a multicultural, multilingual, international church with strong clergy leadership whose identity is expressed in liturgical worship, prayers for the world, and the holy communion service, and that is filled with children, laughter and love for each other, and is in ministry to and with the community that surrounds our church.[18]

LIVING INTO AMBIGUITY

Worship at Northwoods follows the lectionary. Each Sunday morning a different child, youth, or adult reads each lesson. Winston Worrell, the youth minister, usually leads the congregation in the reading of the psalm from the hymnal. People are encouraged to read along in the bibles placed in the pew racks. As we participated in the worship of this congregation over the year, this ritual activity became increasingly paradigmatic of another theme in the view of church we had begun to experience. Members of these congregations increasingly expect to encounter the working of the Holy Spirit most poignantly at the intersections of their diversity—at those places where the multiplicity of experience and background limits mutual understanding and mutual appreciation—in the liminal spaces where mutual understanding is often impossible to achieve and community is dependent on the presence of the mystery of God.

The practice of lectionary readings in this congregation confronts the newcomer with more than the multiplicity of its voices, which are old and young, female and male, originating in several different nations and regions of the country. The accents and rhythms range from southern drawls to the overlays of other linguistic patterns for those who speak English as a second language. Sometimes people strain to hear through the reticent soft-spokenness of a child suddenly shy or the struggle of adults to articulate the English words. The translation of the Bible on the pulpit and in the pews is the Revised Standard Version. Most read, however, from their personal bibles, which on any given Sunday morning may include the King James, the Living, and the New Revised Standard Version (which the pastor usually uses except when he turns to the Good News Bible for some reading from the Pauline letters). Some readers couch their reading with sensitivity to gender inclusiveness. Others do not. Some readers reach the end of the passage and stop, while others add a liturgical conclusion, sometimes calling for a congregational response. The range of interpretive traditions, cultural perspectives, and personal commitments behind these choices are not discussed. Nothing in the worship bulletin indicates for the worshiper what might be expected. Members of the congregation do not seem to perceive anything irregular or discordant about this mixture of rhythms, texts, and responses—even when they cannot quite predict what will happen next or complain that they could not understand the reader. Quite the contrary, this ritual pattern may dramatize not only the celebration of differences church members honor among themselves but their willingness to live into the ambiguity arising from the gaps among those differences.

Voluntary associations (which include congregations in the Protestant traditions) traditionally cope with the ambiguity arising from the encounters of difference by creating a variety of groups to give special attention to the range of diversity in an organization. This allows a congregation or any other voluntary society to accept the presence of diverse values, beliefs, and practices without requiring people to negotiate them on a continuing basis. It creates a pattern of collegiality for those most "like us" inside the group, and a pattern of tolerance for those least like us outside the group. One of the most obvious examples of these patterns in most Protestant congregations in the United States may be seen in the separation of age groups in congregational education. The notion of a generation gap between youth and adults underscores a societal assumption regarding the difficulty of meaningful communication across generational lines. Most congregations further limit the potential experience of ambiguity in their programmatic and administrative structures by dividing leadership responsibilities in ways that give preference to career and personal interests. Hence, bankers tend to be on finance and trustee committees and social workers on social-justice committees. Beyond the congregation this strategy for coping with the ambiguity emerging from the encounter with difference has contributed to the division of Protestant Christian communities along denominational, social class, racial, and political ideology lines. This strategy has allowed people to be quite tolerant of beliefs, values, and practices in the larger community as long as they fall within the orbit of denominational self-understanding[19] or in the larger community within a generally Christian and republican notion of the worth and responsibility of the individual and the freedom of association.

As Iris Marion Young has pointed out, the effect of this social strategy is "to reduce differences to unity"[20] in the concreteness of organizational life. Examples dominate discussions of Protestant church organizational life. In the nineteenth century, for example, church leaders concerned about the dangers to civilization on the frontier of the nation organized several cooperative societies, such as the American Sunday School Union and the American Tract Society, to spread literacy and to nurture citizenship and discipleship. A basic premise in each of these collaborative efforts was the agreement that they would not publish or promote anything offensive to any member party. Differences in theology, liturgy, mission, and even cultural heritage could be accepted only as long as they did not contaminate the common enterprise. The persistent struggle over the place and role of religion in public schools grows out of a similar quest to avoid anything controversial in the education of religiously diverse peoples. When Protestants dominated the public school establishment, tenuous agreements permitting certain passages of scripture to be read and certain prayers to be recited fell apart when other religious and nonreligious groups correctly claimed that such an approach to religion did not respect or honor their traditions or values. Since religion proved controversial, many schools across the country declared it did not belong in the classroom.

Congregational life followed a similar premise, except, unlike the public school, which provided only one tuition-free option in a community, people could choose from several congregations and denominations. Covenants and membership vows provided explicit statements for the boundaries of interpreting traditions and beliefs. Management models emphasizing efficiency and orderliness in decision-making and in teaching established frameworks to guide congregational life and learning. Both efforts limited the potential for experiencing ambiguity in matters of belief and organizational life. With a few exceptions, such as the Church of All Nations organized by Howard Thurman, voluntary approaches to American U.S. Protestant church life have explicitly sought to avoid the experience of ambiguity that occur when differences of race, culture, gender, class, and age are taken seriously. Consequently, church people (men more so than women) in the nation generally have experienced considerable freedom to be Christians in particular communities organized along those lines but not to live out of the particularity of their religious convictions and values in communities of faith embracing religious and other kinds of difference.[21]

Voluntary associations are based on the premise that while difference is integral to the nature of reality, human beings can only tolerate a certain range of diversity in their own associations and experience. These congregations challenge that notion by shifting the location of the experience of ambiguity from outside to inside congregational life in the daily negotiations over the content and practices of worship, business, education, and mission.[22] The experience of ambiguity does not lead to discomfort or even alienation for the people of these churches; instead, it contributes to a sense of expectancy regarding the work of the Holy Spirit in their midst. The embrace of difference, consequently, involves the dynamics of living expectantly into the possibilities of encountering the grace of God at the points where the encounters of difference seem fraught with ambiguity.

The dynamics of living into ambiguity as a primary source to meaning and faith involve at least four elements. The first builds on the insight of C. A. Bowers and David Flinders that a school classroom actually functions as an "ecology of language processes and cultural patterns." A similar claim might be made for congregations. This ecology consists of practices of spoken and written speech, the way personal and social space is organized and used, "the body language of movement, posture, and facial expression."[23] We suggest that this ecological perspective also includes the interplay of varied world views or belief systems that shape and give impetus to the ways diverse members in a community perceive and make sense of their experience of the others around them, the life of the community itself, and the range of responsivity to be found among diverse peoples to the gracious activity of God. A major shift may be discerned in these congregations. The quest to reduce differences by privileging certain language processes, cultural patterns, or belief systems is diminished. Instead, the pastors and several lay leaders redirect their attention to listening and responding to each other through and across those differences. This often happens in and through individual conversation. It occurs as significantly during committee meetings, covered dish dinners, while listening to a variety of voices and texts in the liturgy, and during a pageant celebrating some event in the church year. From this vantage point particularity becomes a catalyst to creativity in the congregation as a whole.

A second dynamic of living into ambiguity in the nurture of faith and meaning centers on the communication patterns of the congregations. The quest integral to speaking and listening across the diversities in these congregations shifts the emphasis in conversation from a quest for norms in doctrine, method, and practice to the quest to empower the voices of all who participate.[24] Letty Russell's image of the church as a "community of anticipation" perhaps most accurately catches this dynamic. The tasks are clear: "building confidence in God's love as a community of faith; building commitment to live out the story of God's liberating action as a community of freedom; and building knowledge of the story and its future promise."[25] The dynamics of expectation become explicit as each congregation listens carefully to the voices of children and youth as agents of good news. Children and youth are encouraged to speak in church—reading scripture, responding to a children's sermon in worship, writing scripts and producing skits for worship and fellowship dinners, voting on congregational decisions. Empowered, spirit-filled speaking—including that done by children—promotes confidence and skill. Perhaps the most consistently dramatic example of empowered speech and energized listening occurs during the time of sharing at Oakhurst, described earlier. Persons of all ages are encouraged to speak. Forms of speaking range from testimonials to requests for prayer, to exhortations, to song. Perhaps the most common example of empowered listening and speaking occurred whenever Rev. Martha in an almost ritualistic manner, and numerous other people in more informal ways, assumed responsibility for reporting an idea or thought they had heard and then requesting other people to articulate their views on the matter. This rich sharing of information gathers up and builds out of the contributions of all who speak. The views that emerge from this process, however, cannot function normatively. New voices interrupt that process. Their perspectives must be gathered into the continuing process of building up the life of the community. Otherwise some voices would inevitably be pushed to the margins or silenced rather than nurtured and encouraged. New events create new conditions for uncertainty and ambiguity. Instead of being interruptions and intrusions, however, in the embrace of difference they become new opportunities for communication in the congregation's quest to discern the work of the Spirit in its midst.

A third dynamic emerging from the effort to live into the ambiguity that arises through encounters with difference involves an increasing capacity for what Sharon Welch has called "mutual critique." In these exchanges among diverse persons the balance of power in their conversations moves from a hierarchical to a horizontal relationship. The pattern may be most evident at Cedar Grove when Rev. Martha takes an idea she has heard in the congregation or community, gives it a place in the community's conversation, ensures that it is heard and examined among the various constituencies of the congregation, and shares the critiques emerging from these conversations. If the idea continues to have merit, it is then rearticulated to reflect the larger conversation before being brought to a vote in a meeting. This process permeates the worship service, committee meetings, fellowship times, and informal conversations in people's homes and the parking lot. A similar dynamic might be seen in the workings of the Oakhurst session, especially in the candid exchanges between Nibs and Inez Fleming, an African-American elder of the congregation. Together they model the mutuality of sharing and critique that emerges when European American and African American trust each other enough in the integrity of their differences to probe fully the strengths and limits of each other's ideas and thoughts on a subject. Differences are aired, examined, and assessed. Conflicts do occur, but they do not seem to interrupt the vitality of the mutuality in these congregations as long as 1) people have taken the time to listen to each other to the point they can begin to recognize the extent of the differences that separate them; 2) leaders recognize that any decision requires the contribution of all ages and groups to the exploration of issues (often in a variety of cultural styles of interaction); and 3) the differences contributing to the conflict become clues to some new insight into the work of God's spirit.

A fourth dynamic involved in living into the ambiguity arising from the embrace of difference occurs in the contrasting movements of gathering up people's shared perspectives and practices and honoring the diverse gifts of each person and constituent group. We have already noted how these congregations strive to overcome the assimilationist patterns of social cohesion, and yet each does seek to have a distinctive identity and mission. They do engage their members in rigorous efforts to retrieve and live into the traditions of Christian faith—even if often from the margins of that tradition's corporate memory. They affirm in this process the impulse to cultural embeddedness so crucial to the continuity of communities across the generations. The efforts to project a shared vision to guide their ministries led Oakhurst and Northwoods to go through lengthy discussions directed to the writing of mission statements. The liturgy of each congregation provides a shared perspective on the relationship of faith and daily life, but worshipers expect to be surprised by variations in content, form, and experience from week to week.

At the same time these congregations endorse in a variety of ways the counter-impulse to differentiation along lines of culture, gender, class, and/or sexual orientation. At times this movement is institutionalized, as in Oakhurst's two choirs and the differences in format and approach to worship on the fourth Sunday when the Mass Choir sings. In some respects this process is most evident in informal ways in the new cultural encounters at Northwoods. Worship, for example, is the one time during the week when its African members can wear traditional clothes. The presence of new cultures led long-time European-American members to begin to talk about their origins in Oklahoma, Montana, or south Alabama. One among this group, originally from Panama, decided maybe she was really brown and not white. As we were completing this book, several Liberian members decided it was time to introduce other members of the congregation to their own traditional handshake. So the repertoire of practices of greeting in this congregation now extend beyond the traditional "hug, shake, or kiss" to include a handshake that concludes with a snap of the fingers. In this way cultural diversity increases and enriches the complexity of the patterns of hospitality integral to the life of the congregation.

SUMMARY

The three churches in this study reveal in their life and work a commitment to the principle of volunteerism that informs the polity of historically mainline Protestant churches in the United States. This commitment is evident in the particularistic mission of each congregation to embrace racial and cultural diversity in a social environment that privileges racial and cultural homogeneity in Christian faith communities. Despite the establishment of bonds linking people across generational, racial, cultural, and class lines (especially at Oakhurst), these congregations assume individuals will voluntarily choose to join, stay, or leave their corporate life. Perhaps not surprisingly, they locate the sources to these views in biblical notions of covenant and salvation, which emphasize the responsibility of individuals in relation to God and each other.

Yet, the embrace of difference does alter their view of church. This new view of church shifts congregational praxis from living out of the implications of authoritative doctrines and structures inherited from the past to the interplay of an examination of the congregation's context and the possibilities for congregational identity and mission to be found in memories of the future transmitted through scripture and tradition. The ambiguity arising from the encounters of people who discover they cannot fully understand or appreciate each other becomes the context for a praxis of multiplicity. This praxis gathers diverse peoples into communities of anticipation—filled with wonder over the creativity of God's spirit in their midst. Since the relationships in congregations embracing diversity tend to be fluid and changing, their status or structure can never be assumed. The task of building up the church as the body of Christ—a metaphor used frequently in all three churches—never ends. The ministry of building community involves negotiating local relationships and structures. It celebrates the distinctive negotiations among diverse peoples in that local setting. From this perspective it takes all the different people "to be the church together."

Notes

1. After the completion of our study, the Spanish-speaking ministry pulled out of Northwoods. Although linguistic issues continued to be a major struggle, this decision had more to do with the confluence of the desire of the leadership of the Spanish-speaking ministry to have more authority for the ministry and to the lack of support they received, due in part, to the tensions women experienced when they encountered the macho dynamics in the male pastor's leadership style. This is one of several instances in our study in which cultural and gender values conflicted. During a long meeting of prayer and Bible study, an expanded Administrative Council reconfirmed its intent to be a multilingual as well as multicultural congregation.

2. C. Peter Wagner, *Our Kind of People: The Ethical Dimensions of Church Growth in America* (Richmond: John Knox Press, 1979), 4.

3. Letty M. Russell, *The Future of Partnership* (Philadelphia: The Westminster Press, 1979), 54.

4. Letty M. Russell, *Church in the Round: Feminist Interpretation of the Church* (Louisville: Westminster/John Knox Press, 1993), 43.

5. Elizabeth Schüssler Fiorenza, *Discipleship of Equals: A Critical Feminist Ekklesia-logy of Liberation* (New York: Crossroad Publishing Company, 1993), 104-16.

6. Sharon Welch, "An Ethic of Solidarity and Difference," in *Postmodernism, Feminism, and Cultural Politics: Redrawing Educational Boundaries*, ed. Henry A. Giroux (Albany: State University of New York Press, 1991), 83.

7. Margaret Wheatley, in a study of leadership from the perspective of the "new science," has explored this notion of *belonging* under the rubric of a sense of ownership for the life and mission of an organization. She notes that it conveys a sense of the emotional investment people bring to

their participation in the organization. As such, it is a primary source of energy for the work of the organization. In these congregations, this sense of *ownership* is often so intense that the common church complaint about not finding volunteers is rarely heard. Instead, a significant core of volunteers in each congregation runs the risk of burn-out from the deep investment in the congregation's mission (*Leadership and the New Science: Learning About Organization from an Orderly Universe* [San Francisco: Berrett-Loehler Publishers, 1992], 66).

8. The resulting ambiguity may be illustrated by the tendency among African Americans outside the church to identify Cedar Grove as a *white* congregation and among European Americans, to identify it as a *black* congregation. In contrast, Cedar Grove members say it encompasses both.

9. The image of a community of equals is developed more fully in Charles D. Blakeney and Ronnie A.F. Blakeney, "Pluralism and the Dilemma of Discordance among Blacks and Jews," in *The Challenge of Pluralism: Education, Politics, and Values,* ed. F. Clark Power and Daniel K. Lapsley (Notre Dame, IN: University of Notre Dame Press, 1992); see also Schüssler Fiorenza, who explores the political dynamics in this metaphor we also intend in our usage of "a community of equals." She argues against the efforts of persons who call for access and integration into "patriarchal"— and, we would add, racist—"structures." She seeks instead to "articulate *ekklesia* as a *discipleship of equals* that can make present the *baseileia,* the alternative world of justice and well-being intended by the life-giving power of G-d as reality and vision in the midst of the death-dealing powers of patriarchal oppression and dehumanization" (11-12).

10. Russell, *The Future of Partnership,* 54-59.

11. Henry A. Giroux, drawing on the work of Emily Hicks, identifies and critiques some of the primary themes in contemporary postmodern theory. It challenges, he notes, the emphasis in modernist culture to negate "the possibility of identities created within the experience of multiple narratives and 'border' crossings"; critiques the extent to which "European culture becomes identified with the center of civilization" rather than as one among many cultural traditions; calls into question the definition of "high culture" in "essentialist terms" and the preferential treatment it receives in education; and challenges the tendency to view "history" as "critical memory," thereby focusing meaning, rather than to see it as "a proliferation of images" expanding consciousness to a range of possible meanings ("Introduction: Modernism, Postmodernism, and Feminism: Rethinking the Boundaries of Educational Discourse," *in Postmodernism, Feminism, and Cultural Politics: Redrawing Educational Boundaries,* ed. Henry A. Giroux [Albany: State University of New York Press, 1991], 22).

12. Robert Schreiter, *Constructing Local Theologies* (Maryknoll, NY: Orbis Books, 1986), 4-5.

13. Ibid., 22-23.

14. Letty M. Russell, *Household of Freedom: Authority in Feminist Theology* (Philadelphia: The Westminster Press, 1987), 30.

15. Russell, *The Future of Partnership*, 82.

16. Ibid., 34-35.

17. Although Jerome had prepared six questions, time permitted only three to be discussed: "When have you felt good about being a member of Northwoods?" "When you brag about Northwoods, what do you say?" "When/where has our church expressed or witnessed to the vitality of the Spirit?"

18. From the Northwoods weekly newsletter.

19. This pattern is collapsing as denominational loyalty gives way to congregational loyalty. The Search Institute study *Effective Christian Education: A National Study of Protestant Congregations* points to the increasing proliferation of theological and faith patterns among people within the same denomination and the shift in loyalty from denomination to congregation. This allows for much greater diversity among congregations in matters of belief and communal practice than in the past ([Minneapolis: Search Institute, 1990], 16-20).

20. Iris Marion Young, *Justice and the Politics of Difference* (Princeton: Princeton University Press, 1990), 97.

21. Stephen L. Carter has most recently explored this dynamic in American U.S. life. He argues that "in our zeal to keep religion from dominating our politics, we have created a political and legal culture that presses the religiously faithful to be other than themselves, to act publicly, and sometimes privately as well, as though their faith does not matter to them" (*The Culture of Disbelief: How American Law and Politics Trivialize Religious Devotion* [New York: Basicbooks, 1993], 3).

22. The implications of accepting ambiguity as context for the processes of knowing and nurturing faith are developed further in chapter 7.

23. C. A. Bowers and David J. Flinders, *Responsive Teaching: An Ecological Approach to Classroom Patterns of Language, Culture, and Thought* (New York: Teachers College Press, 1990), 2.

24. This shift in the focus of attention from the transmission of doctrine to the empowerment of speech has some similarities to the argument Rebecca Chopp makes in *The Power to Speak: Feminism, Language, God*. When the language of theology belongs to a hierarchical patriarchy, the people on the margins are not empowered to participate in the proclamation of the Word. We see in these churches preliminary struggles to empower children, women, and persons who by reason of race, culture, or class have had to proclaim their experience of God from the margins of human community, to engage in practices of what Chopp calls "emancipatory transformation" ([New York: The Crossroad Publishing Company, 1991], 4).

25. Letty M. Russell, *Growth in Partnership* (Philadelphia: The Westminster Press, 1981), 104-5.

6

CONGREGATIONAL EDUCATION

Forming Community

Sierra Leone M. is a very small girl who has been named for a very small country in Africa. That is where we come in, for it is in our nurture of her that she will be nurtured into the family of God.
—Words spoken on the occasion of Sierra Leone's baptism.

INTRODUCTION

During one of our final sessions in the churches an active European-American laywoman began to talk about the next level of issues facing her congregation as it attempted to draw upon its diversity as a resource for its life and mission. She observed that the music of the congregation's worship was "still too white. It doesn't reflect the heritage or experience of our black church members." A few years earlier this same woman had reportedly walked out of a church meeting because it voted to rent space to a black Seventh Day Adventist congregation, saying it was like "letting Niggers into your living room." An African-American woman in another congregation shared with us her own pilgrimage out of distrust for white folks to the conviction that the future of the church and nation depends on the ability to collaborate across differences. We saw many other signs of the influence of the ministries of these congregations in people's lives. A young woman locates the impetus for her quest to improve the education children receive in the local schools to her congregation's commitment to stabilize the community. Despite their struggles over the maintenance of the Sunday schools, children in each congregation demonstrate a high degree of familiarity with biblical narratives and the liturgical practices of the congregation. Lay leaders in each congregation make use of an emerging shared theological vocabulary to describe their life together and mission in the community.

Lawrence Cremin, in an oft-quoted definition of education, notes that it involves the "deliberate, systematic, and sustained effort" of a family, community, or society "to transmit, evoke, or acquire knowledge, values, attitudes, skills, or sensibilities" it deems crucial to the maintenance and renewal of its common life.[1] Education consists of the formal efforts of a community to socialize into membership those born into the community or those who have chosen to enter into its identity. In a commentary on *Habits of the Heart*, C. A. Bowers explores the difficulty of this task for contemporary education. "The language of individualism," which dominates much of the national consciousness, "limits our ability to understand our embeddedness" in what Bellah and his colleagues called a "social ecology"—the structure of relationships and processes that support and sustain community. Community, which is the object of any education, is further undermined by the increasing concentration of wealth "in the hands of a privileged few, by distortions in the work place, and by the progressive corruption of the democratic process." The power dynamics of cultural, racial, and economic pluralism have only exacerbated the fragility of education in religious communities and society. Bowers, therefore, calls for a commitment to education directed to the restoration of community.[2]

Typically people in the United States associate these "deliberate, systematic, and sustained" efforts to maintain, restore, or renew ecclesial or public communities with some form of schooling. In Protestant churches the Sunday school and related formal study and catechetical programs have been seen as primary agencies of congregational education. Weekday schools extend the strategy for many Catholics, Lutherans, and more recently, many Protestant congregations. In each of the congregations in this study a strong Sunday school tradition exists. Some people continue to look to the Sunday school as a primary agency for teaching and learning. We perceive, however, that their educational strengths lie elsewhere. Except for two adult classes at Northwoods, membership in the three Sunday schools has declined over the years and attendance is sporadic. Teachers are difficult to recruit. Church leaders have difficulty finding curriculum resources considered relevant to the mission and contexts of these congregations.

At the same time, learning is obviously taking place—indeed, highly focused learning. In this chapter we seek to explore the character of the education emerging from the quest in each congregation to nurture among its members a sense of identity and mission that distinctively embraces racial and cultural diversity. That quest has required each congregation to reassess its assumptions about how it educates, because it is engaged in fashioning a new kind of faith community. Those engaged in this task find few precedents for their efforts in either church or public education. Further, they find few resources helpful to the task they have set before themselves.[3] They share in the quests to maintain or even restore traditional notions of congregational community, but find themselves engaged more clearly in the effort to creating a new kind of community out of those traditions.

"THE OLD WAYS DO NOT WORK FOR US"

A walk down the hall of the children's floor of the educational building at Northwoods takes one back at least fifteen years—when it still had the feel of being new. Large spacious rooms, sturdy birch top tables and chairs in age-appropriate sizes, child-eye level bulletin boards, coat hooks, and storage shelves all indicate familiarity with the highest standards educators proposed for outfitting rooms. In the church school office, cupboards hold paper (some of it faded), crayons (mostly in broken pieces), old tempura paint powder that no longer dissolves in water, faded costumes, three shelves of children's books published before 1985, and a well-organized filing system for the pictures and maps that accompanied curriculum resources printed before that date. Pictures from this file posted on the wall by current teachers reveal the artistic styles in denominational curriculum resources of the period. A filing cabinet reveals meticulous record-keeping systems for attendance and giving. The five large classrooms could easily accommodate more than one hundred children. For several years the hallway was almost silent. Now as many as twenty children might be in attendance. But teachers who worked in those rooms in the past feel increasing frustration over the gap between their assumptions about how teaching and learning should take place and the reality of their experience.

They expected to meet new challenges from the linguistic diversity they encountered in the children now attending. But they did not expect to be frustrated about the perceived inappropriateness of denominational curriculum resources. For Cedar Grove and Oakhurst the standard resources were "awfully white." For Northwoods the resources provided no clues for teachers working in the bilingual classroom. Caroline Leach, Oakhurst's associate pastor and a professional Christian educator, noted gender, class, and race biases as well as the irrelevance of much curricular content to the life issues of children, youth, and adults seeking to live out of the Christian tradition into the justice and peace issues of urban life. Caroline spends much of her energy looking for books with stories and units of study that might be adapted to the local situation. She also edits the words in existing resources and colors in the pictures to reflect more adequately the image of church Oakhurst seeks to foster. No one fills a similar role in the other two congregations.

Denominational leadership-training workshops seem equally irrelevant to the teachers and leaders in these congregations. Usually they are dismissed because "they don't speak to our needs." When probed, this phrase usually means these workshops do not address issues of difference in learning and cultural perspective. For some, like Caroline, they do not give appropriate attention to the justice and social issues at the heart of the class, race, and gender practices in the church and country. This "dis-ease" with traditional educational structures and assumptions among members of these congregations reflects general critiques of education in the church and nation.

As long ago as 1970 John Westerhoff pointed out limitations of the Sunday school as an agency for forming faith in congregational life.

> In a day of anxiety and frustration about the Christian education of children and youth, we hope for a beefed-up church school. We spend large sums of money on new educational plants; we redesign the content to be taught; we develop new curricular resources, and increase the use of new media; we devise methods for teacher education, hire professional leadership, expand our church school programs, and reorganize our school environment. We explore and develop new teaching methods such as individualized instruction, teaching machines, team teaching, ungraded classes, homogeneous grouping, independent study and the like. We try ecumenical schools and weekday classes.

These attempts at reform in church education are not in themselves going to meet our educational needs. What is demanded is a major shift in emphasis from schooling to education, i.e., all the ways a person learns.[4]

As a student of C. Ellis Nelson, Westerhoff's awareness of the ways the entire community of faith contributes to the nurture of the "faith we live by" had been heightened. Faith, Nelson had asserted, "is communicated by a community of believers" and the "meaning of faith is developed by its members out of their history, by their interaction with each other, and in relation to the events that take place in their lives."[5] As an astute observer of Protestant ecclesial life in the nation, Westerhoff called church leaders to look beyond the collapsing partnership of family, church Sunday school, and public school (an institutional configuration that Robert Lynn had called the American U.S. Protestant strategy of education) for new ways to talk about religious education in the church and nation.[6] Westerhoff recognized earlier than most that the Sunday school simply could not carry the full load of this task of nurturing faith for the sake of the church. He did not explore the dilemma facing the congregations in our study regarding the challenge of cultural and racial diversity to that same educational tradition. The Protestant educational strategy of family, church, and school drew upon such metaphors as the "melting pot" to underscore its commitment to socialization strategies of assimilation into what Lawrence Cremin has described as the English mold for American U.S. identity. Cremin concluded that in the working out of this educational strategy "the prevailing assumption was clear: people could be educated to transcend the barriers of ethnicity and religion in order to become full-fledged members of the American community, but they could not be educated to transcend the barriers of race."[7] The dilemma for the education in these congregations, of course, grows out of their commitment to reject the notion that race is a barrier to community in the church or nation. For Oakhurst the issue is even more explicit. The notion of a society ordered on the values and perspectives of a homophobic and Eurocentric middle class for national and ecclesial identity must be challenged as idolatrous.

The "dis-ease" in these three congregations moves beyond the discussion of the limits of the Sunday school as a primary educational strategy for fashioning a community of diversity. It also illumines the growing challenge among many educators to the cultural, class, and gender biases in the pedagogical practices to be found in the dynamics of teaching and learning. As such, the more recent critique moves beyond the insensitivity to age or developmental patterns, which has been well-addressed by such educational innovators as Johann Pestalozzi in the nineteenth century, through the early twentieth-century reformist efforts of Maria Montessori and John Dewey, and in the more recent research and writing of Jean Piaget, Erik Erikson, Lawrence Kohlberg, Carol Gilligan, and James Fowler.[8]

Jonathan Kozol and Paulo Freire have been among the most widely read critics of what happens between teachers and students. Kozol, perhaps more than anyone, has brought into public consciousness "savage inequalities" in the nation's schools based on race and the distribution of economic resources (one wonders what one might find if a similar study were made of the education in churches). Brazilian educator Freire's passionate analysis of the way education helps to sustain the economic and political ideologies of the powerful has inspired a whole new generation of scholarship in education.[9] Freire focused attention on ways educators (often unconsciously) engage in the social, political, and economic domination of students by "stimulating their credulity" to accept a "world of oppression"— indeed, contribute to the conditions of their own oppression.

This issue became real at Northwoods for two high school students. One, born in Liberia, struggled with what it means to be black in the United States. As an African he had little self-consciousness about claiming that his skin color was black, but as a newcomer to this country he struggled with the imposition he experienced from both white and black peers and teachers to live out of the history of the oppression of slavery, segregation, and prejudice of African Americans into an ideology of "blackness." The other, a European American, transferred high schools after he decided his classroom performance had been adversely affected by harassment from students in the school's dominant racial group—in this instance, African Americans.

Freire explored ways educational practices and structures collude in the oppression of students. When teachers assume they know what students need to know rather than help them develop power "to perceive critically the way they exist in the world with which and in which they find themselves," Freire contended, they perpetuate student self-perceptions of their own powerlessness. They see "the world as a static reality," rather than as "a reality in process" or in transformation. They do not provide an appropriate "space"—one characterized by openness, clear boundaries, and hospitality—for students such as the two young men mentioned above to work out critical issues of identity and community raised in the encounter of diverse cultures and classes.[10]

Freire's concern had to do with ways education contributed to the persistence of economic and political disparity between the haves and have-nots of a nation. As a staff member of the World Council of Churches his concern extended to ways religious education participates in the ideological oppression of the poor and marginal members of a community. The research of Mary Field Belenky and her colleagues pushes that critique to include ways pedagogical practices emphasizing hierarchy and linearity silence the voices of women. A growing number of scholars have begun to spell out some of the elements in culturally distinctive patterns of learning—an issue of great practical concern to the teachers in these three congregations.[11]

The tension the teachers and leaders in these three congregations encounter in an especially dramatic way grows out of the limits of the educational strategies inherited from the past. These limits continue to dominate their thinking about how to incorporate their increasing sensitivity to the plurality of cultural and ideological perspectives to be found among their constituencies. The dynamics of teaching and learning they are discovering, are not neutral—a point Michael Apple and others have made. Neither does neutrality extend to gender, race, ethnicity, social class, or theological perspective.[12] Educational strategies of assimilation ultimately demean someone. Consequently, any education that embraces and affirms diversity engages teachers and learners in "transgressing" boundaries integral to those differences to the point that students and teachers might interrogate, as bell hooks has suggested, the biases in curriculum and educational institutions that contribute to the domination, oppression, or marginalization of any group or groups among them.[13]

FORMING COMMUNITY: ORIGINATING EDUCATIONAL TASK OR A PLURALISTIC CONGREGATION IN A PLURALISTIC WORLD

Maria Harris has described education as the work of fashioning community. It shifts the metaphorical focus of our attention from traditional notions of education as "transmitting" or from John Dewey's image of education as "reconstructing" or "reorganizing experience." Its aesthetic possibilities become evident in the biblical prophet's image of a potter giving shape to a pot. The process is a dynamic one of forming and reforming toward the artist's vision of the vessel being created. Its qualities are more closely aligned with

St. Paul's image of the work of the church as "building up" or giving life to the community.[14] The process is pre-eminently theological—redefining and redirecting congregational identity and mission in which personal faith and mission might be nurtured.

The challenge before these congregations, however, occurs in developing an educational process that seeks not communal homogeneity but communal heterogeneity.[15] Although the schools of the nation have been struggling with this task since Brown *vs.* Topeka in 1954, few precedents exist in church educational practice to guide their efforts. In their education, in other words, the fragility of the future of these congregations becomes most visible. How does one maintain or renew community life, when its shape is in some respects just being formed? How does one pass on traditions allocated in most congregations to the margins of their corporate experience? What is the character of the transmissive and transformative processes of teaching and learning when education traditionally emphasizes the maintenance of borders? How does education celebrate difference when it traditionally seeks to collapse social boundaries and cultural markers highlighting them? A closer examination of congregational practices illumines at least four resources to forming communities of diversity in and through the education of these congregations: 1) event-centered ecologies giving order and purpose to the common life of the congregation and its relation to the larger community; 2) the quest to read ancient texts from inside the situation of the diversity of their common lives; 3) the struggle to alter the dynamics of power among alternative ways of living and being together; and 4) a corporate methodology for theological reflection.

An Event-Centered Educational Ecology

Worship provides the frame and impetus to congregational identity and mission in these three congregations. The processes contributing to congregational identity originate in and are renewed (and sometimes transformed) in and through the repeated gathering of each congregation for worship on Sunday morning and at other significant times of the liturgical year. Despite significant differences in the ways these three congregations embody church, several clues underscore the centrality of worship in their education. Average attendance at worship is consistently higher than that found in most mainstream Protestant churches—ranging from approximately 50 percent of members who were not housebound at Cedar Grove, to nearly 60 percent at Northwoods, and often approaching 75 percent at Oakhurst. Worship is intensely intergenerational—not only in the

presence of children and youth, but in the assumption in each congregation that children and youth have an important place and role
in the leadership of worship. Unlike many mainline Protestant
churches of comparable size, these congregations do not have a core
group of people who limit their participation on Sunday mornings
to the Sunday school. Instead, most people regularly move out of
their Sunday school classrooms into the worship service. Mission
priorities are introduced, gain momentum through the interpretations of congregational leaders, and gather up people to move out
into the community during the worship hour. Although newsletters,
congregational committees, and informal conversational networks
are important vehicles for communicating congregational concerns
and for congregational instruction, most important information is
shared and interpreted during the weekly gathering for worship.
Accounts of the concerns of the congregation—both personal and
missional—are woven into the liturgy of worship. Primary interpretations of congregational programs and mission activities are made.
Lay leaders and pastors give theological analyses of the conditions
that give impetus to mission activities during times for special announcements or during the sermon itself. If we include the conversations at Cedar Grove before and after the worship service, the worship
hour in each of these congregations lasts from ninety minutes in all
three churches to more than two hours on rare occasions at Oakhurst.

Three characteristics of worship underscore its educative influence on the life and mission of these three congregations. Perhaps
most noticeable to the first time visitor are the rites of incorporation
and intensification. Rituals of baptism are not relegated to the *end*
of the hour at Oakhurst but become instead a primary focus for the
gathered congregation's attention. New members at Northwoods are
surrounded by a Sunday school class or other group in the congregation to indicate the extent of the fellowship and support that surrounds them. The intimate interdependence of congregants is
underscored at Oakhurst when the concerns of the congregation are
shared and at Northwoods when the congregation joins the pastor
around the communion table for prayers for church members, the
community, city, country, and world. The ritual of greeting at
Oakhurst erupts as people move throughout the sanctuary in a burst
of hugging and handshaking among persons of all ages that may last
ten minutes or more. Following the benediction, members of
Northwoods are invited to give each other "a hug, a kiss, or a handshake," and the time of meeting and greeting that follows lasts thirty
minutes or more. The time for conversation at Cedar Grove before

and after worship is perhaps even more leisurely and intimate. Especially on Sundays when guests are present Cedar Grove folk line up outside the door to greet them as if they were visiting dignitaries. The repetition of these rituals clearly contributes to the sense of mutuality and intimacy across lines of race, ethnicity, gender, and generation in all three churches and across the boundaries of sexual orientation and class at Oakhurst as well.

A second characteristic of the event of worship as the originating impulse to congregational education in these congregations may be traced to its role in establishing a shared vocabulary for naming and interpreting their own experiences within the course of Christian tradition. That vocabulary tends to be familial and informal at Cedar Grove. It introduces into reformed theological traditions an explicitly anti-racist rhetoric at Oakhurst. It establishes a framework for discussions at Northwoods about its corporate identity and mission in an increasingly cross-cultural appropriation of the communal ecclesial language rooted in prayer and scripture. The longer experience of Oakhurst and Cedar Grove may provide a clue to the amazing extent to which these relatively new vocabularies of faith are shared.

Congregants approach worship in these congregations with what we considered an amazingly high degree of expectation. We often heard someone say to us when talking about their church, "You never know quite what to expect here." Actually the liturgical structure in each congregation is quite consistent from week to week. Within this framework surprises happen—moments that experientially ground congregational learning. These surprises can occur through the sharing of leadership in worship. Although the pastors are each consistently involved, many other people have important roles. During our second visit to Oakhurst, for example, the youth planned the worship service, which included a frank and candid skit they had written on sexuality in teen culture. The subject matter and language would have been censored on television and in most schools of the city. One family did remove its children from the sanctuary. The youth, however, felt no constraints in their efforts to engage the social realities of their lives with their understanding of the gospel. We have already emphasized the role of children in leading worship. The initiative for their leadership is as likely to come from a member of the church as from one of the pastors.

These surprises occur just as often in the efforts of the leaders of worship to respond to the diversity in the congregations. Musical forms and genres vary. Listening to the ways persons from different cultural backgrounds, classes, or genders experience a given text opens up new interpretations for passages of scripture heretofore considered familiar. This often creates anxiety among worship leaders and some church members, but the resulting gifts are usually identified with the work of the Holy Spirit.

A fourth characteristic of the education centered on the events of worship in these congregations is the emergence of a distinctive ecology of congregational education. The patterns vary. At Cedar Grove fellowship dinners function as the harmonic partner of worship in nurturing congregational relationships and providing a shared context for the congregational conversations that explore and probe the interplay of issues its members face in the community and its quest to make sense of them in light of their Christian heritage. Administrative settings legitimate certain themes and projects. Other gatherings in the church (including volleyball as well as the women's organization) and the community (the P.T.A. and the schools) provide places for further exploration of those themes and projects.

The Sunday school hour at Oakhurst often becomes an occasion for children and youth to prepare for some responsibility in worship. The mission life of the church both gives shape and direction to worship but in turn is interpreted and given momentum through worship. At Oakhurst more than the other two congregations the Session and committees establish a structural framework for the negotiation of differences in the development of policies and programs reflecting the theological vision communicated most clearly through worship. As members move out into the social service and community organizations through which they advocate for the dispossessed and oppressed, they become the worldly contexts for the future nurture of congregational thinking and acting about certain issues.

A shift is occurring in the organizational life of Northwoods directed to issues of faith formation and discipleship training. The nerve center of the congregation used to be in the adult classes of the Sunday school. They provided the leadership, many of the ideas, the work forces, and the primary financial resources to effect the ministries of the church. Increasingly the impetus to ministry and mission seems to occur through the worship service. The committees of the church provide contexts for making strategic decisions about what shall be done and how. Special needs are then taken to the youth and adult Sunday school classes in the quest to find people and resources to work toward the set goals.

In many ways worship as the originating center of congregational identity and mission has the character of an event.[16] We would like to use this term in the sense employed by Robert MacAfee Brown, who noted that all discussions of faith have some relationship to an *event* in the past. These events 1) define "who we are." As we relate to them they have 2) "revelatory significance" for us, giving meaning to who we are and what we do. To the extent that these events define who we are, 3) "we shape our lives in conformity" to their meanings. This conformity is 4) not experienced as "bondage, but liberation." For any event from the past to have the potential to continue to shape our lives and give meaning to them, we 5) "must maintain an ongoing interplay" from our encounters with their meanings from the past, in the present, and into the future.[17] Christians, for example, live out of the *events* of the Exodus, the building of the Davidic kingdom, the exile, and penultimately, the life, death, and resurrection of Jesus Christ. The Christ event is carried through the ages in stories, rituals, structured relationships and institutions, and theological studies. It is enlivened, renewed, and sometimes transformed in the re-enactment of its meanings and relationships by specific people in specific times and places. In that process those events in the past help form and shape contemporary perceptions, perspectives, and practices of individual persons and groups who identify with them. The education, worship, mission, fellowship, and administrative functions of a congregation can never fully gather up the potential meanings and power in its formative events. The dynamics of entering into and taking on the character of the event has the potential to open it up in new ways for the people involved. In that effort congregational life is continuously given shape, purpose, and direction.

In Foster's *Educating Congregations*, four kinds of events are identified. Events such as the life, death, and resurrection of Jesus Christ function as *paradigmatic* events. They establish corporate patterns, standards, and expectations for our lives through the passage of time. They provide the corporate framework for both hearing and living into their stories, rituals, and practices. *Seasonal* events provide a rhythmic structure for remembering and participating in the meanings and experiences of the paradigmatic events that inform us about who we are and to whom we belong. The church year provides a liturgical structure for participation in the narrative structure of those events. Sunday worship functions much like the basic beat to the flow of a congregation's common life. *Occasional* events from mission trips to weddings and baptism intensify and renew and sometimes transform ways in which people relate to paradigmatic events that inform their sense of identity and mission. *Spontaneous* events come as surprises into congregational life and must be taken seriously as threats or possibilities. When their educative potential is seized they too can help shape congregational perspectives and practices. These three congregations witness to the potential transformation of congregational identity when confronted with a changing demographic constituency from which to draw their members.[18]

The pedagogical process emerging from the focus on worship as the impetus and celebration of congregational life and mission involves three steps. In each congregation intense effort is involved in *preparation* for worship. Rarely does the worship leadership include only the pastor, the church secretary who types the bulletin, the choir and its director, and the ushers. Children, youth, and/or adults create banners, arrange flowers, and offer other visual aids. At Cedar Grove and Northwoods acolytes receive weekly instruction for specific responsibilities in that service. Scripture readers are briefed and in some cases trained. On many Sundays music or drama rehearsals precede the worship service. People giving leadership to mission projects prepare interpretive statements. For special celebrations such as the Christmas pageant at Oakhurst or the Pentecost service at Northwoods the cast of persons preparing for worship easily numbers more than half of those who will participate in the service itself.

The act of participation encompasses the dynamics of practice through the repetition of hymns, prayers, and patterns of relating. Northwoods, for example, chooses certain elements of the liturgy to be repeated each week during a liturgical season to enhance its familiarity. At times the concern for practice involves the dynamics of training. Children and youth give leadership in worship at Northwoods and Oakhurst, in part to develop confidence and competence in public roles of ecclesial leadership. The use of a variety of musical forms, art, and drama heightens the role of imagination and affect in the educational process in these congregations.[19]

A third step in event-centered education occurs in the reflection of those involved on the meanings and implications of their experience. This process of local theological reflection is encompassed in the remaining three elements of the congregation's education.

Claiming Tradition from the Margins

The pastors of these congregations explicitly engage members in an exploration of important biblical, theological, and liturgical texts from what some liberation theologians have called the margins or the underside of community life. When Jerome observes in the gathering of the Northwoods congregation around the communion table the scattered "nations and tribes around the throne of the lamb," or when Nibs declares that "breaking down the walls of hostility" is addressed to the fractured relationships of black and white people in Atlanta, Georgia, or when Rev. Martha welcomes a disparate group of persons into the "family" of Cedar Grove, each challenges conventional perspectives on these texts.

The preaching and teaching in these congregations gives evidence to a theme in feminist and liberation hermeneutical discussions. When one begins to approach the sacred texts and practices of a community from the perspective of "the struggles and exegetical concerns of those who are on the periphery of society," those who share experiences of "hunger, sickness, and exploitation" or those who choose to stand in solidarity with people heretofore considered "the other" or "strangers," new insights and interpretations often emerge.[20] This hermeneutical perspective from the margins may be most evident in the preaching of the three congregations. The domination of white European-American scholarship is challenged on a range of issues from the nature and purpose of community life to the meaning of race, gender, and class in God's economy. That preaching is reinforced by the visual imagery of stained-glass windows celebrating the privileged places of persons in God's economy who are traditionally viewed in societies as marginal. At Cedar Grove worshipers gather under images of an adulterous woman, children, and disciples caught in one of their least glorious moments—arguing over who should sit at the right of Jesus in the life to come. The preaching is further reinforced by ritual actions that level hierarchical relationships into circles of friendship for prayer and singing. The shift in the power dynamics of the hermeneutical enterprise in congregational teaching is evident, in other words, in speech and context. The effect lifts the educative process beyond the transmission of culture to what Maxine Greene has described as the demystification of one's own cultural embeddedness. It shifts the location of the educational enterprise from the center of some cultural tradition and perspective to cultural borders. The effect, as David Bailey and Stuart Hall have observed, is that identity is increasingly viewed as "contradictory and . . . always situational." Since black (or white), for example, signifies a "range of experiences," acts representing the meaning of black or white, African American or Korean American involve more than "decentering the subject." It also means exploring "the kaleidoscopic conditions" of the possibilities for meaning to be found in those differences.[21] This process dominated much of the cultural interactions of Northwoods during the time of our study. As increasing numbers of persons joined the congregation, meanings associated with both black and white began to fragment and proliferate. Black not only encompassed a number of African nations and tribes, but Caribbean nations, urban and rural U.S. black experience, northern and southern black experience. White increasingly had to be differentiated among southern Alabama sharecropper experience, urban southern white experience, and the experience of members who began to talk more about their own sense of cultural rootedness on the Great Plains or in New England, Oklahoma, or Canada. An interpretive process that begins in the encounter of difference and is accepted as having potential significance, in other words, heightens congregational expectation to the possibility for significant meanings in diversity that could and have led to transformations of consciousness. This growing sensitivity to local difference creates an openness to discerning differences and new possibilities in scriptural, theological, and liturgical texts. The practice at Northwoods, for example, of envisioning a gathering of the world's nations and tribe around the communion table of their local church in Doraville, Georgia, shatters readings that postpone the realization of this text continuously into some future time.

Altering the Power Dynamics

In a provocative essay on teaching in pluralistic educational settings, C. A. Bowers and David Flinders describe the classroom as "an ecology of language processes and cultural patterns." This metaphor might appropriately be extended to any congregation—perhaps especially to these three congregations. Language processes include both speech and action. The ways various peoples and groups use both personal and social space become integral parts of the message exchange system. The meaning of community at Northwoods, for example, is being negotiated out of quite different cultural modes of human relating and interacting. These assumptions range from a view shared by many African members of the congregation that children are to be supervised by the nearest adult—no matter what his or her relationship to the child—to the ancient Roman notion still influencing the behavior of many European-American adults that children belong to their parents, who are responsible for their care and supervision unless delegated to someone else. The diversity of such assumptions requires continuing negotiations among church members. A range of cultural assumptions about forms of interpersonal address; the meaning of body language, posture, and facial expression; as well as the implications of pitch, tempo, and intensity of speech complicate these negotiations. The dynamics of power at work in a culturally diverse community are intensified, in other words, when efforts at communication convey varied "cultural patterns of thought, behavior, and inner response."[22]

Bowers and Flinders probe this insight. They observe that "not all cultural groups value the same forms of knowledge, and may even diverge in learning styles in ways that reflect differences in cultural views of reality, [which] brings into the open the political nature of the teacher's role." In these congregations, this recognition underscores the political nature of the entire educative process. Which cultural traditions are to be privileged: rural small white church traditions? urban black church traditions? some synthesis of African and American U.S. traditions? Rarely are the political negotiations conscious and direct. They become evident in the persistent and still unsuccessful efforts in the traditional European-American adult Sunday school classes to recruit significant numbers of African-American, African, and Caribbean members into their patterns of teaching and learning in all three churches. They become evident when one member of a team of teachers approaches their common task by drawing on the pedagogical traditions of an African village, which emphasizes the incorporation of children into adult ways of knowing and doing, and another teacher on the team seeks to nurture a sense of autonomy and self-reliance in children by encouraging them to ask questions they can then explore. The tension of expectations between these two teachers is compounded by the African teacher's emphasis on maternal intimacy and the European American's desire to facilitate the nurture of peer relationships.

Several educational theorists have explored the role that education plays in reproducing the ideologies, values, perspectives, and practices of a culture. Others, notably Bowers and Flinders, emphasize the necessity for education to participate in the "restoration of community." In both instances, these writers underscore the role of education in giving shape to or exercising power to influence individual and corporate life. In North American communities seeking to embrace diversity as an integral dimension of their common life, the dynamics in the power to reproduce or to restore community shifts radically. This shift may become evident by contrasting the challenge before these congregations and the task of socializing students into the language processes and cultural patterns of a specific Protestant mainline congregation and denomination. This effort, Bowers observes, exposes "students" to ways to "talk and think about aspects of the cultural group" into which they are being educated. In other words, it provides the vocabulary, linguistic tools, and conceptual framework to reinforce and stabilize the "taken-for-granted" aspects of that cultural experience. If encouraged over the years of a student's educational experience, the student may possess enough perspective and knowledge to reflect on the historical, social, and theological perspectives that give distinctive shape and focus to that cultural experience.[23] In a pluralistic community seeking to discover clues to a vision for the common life of its members from the margins of its disparate traditions, this process takes on a quite different character.

In the first place the presentation of traditions multiplies the options of cultural language processes and patterns available to the educational process. So at Oakhurst the congregational celebration of Christmas includes narratives and ritual practices explicitly rooted in the traditions of Protestant Sunday school Christmas pageants, the Mexican-American Poseda, and the new and emerging traditions of Kwanzaa. Although they are brought together in a single multifaceted event, the sources of the traditions are named and the elements in the traditions are discussed in their own contexts. The ecology of cultural patterns, in other words, becomes the source of multiple narratives in congregational curriculum. The variations in these cultural patterns are not the subject of some objective or phenomenological study. They are engaged as gifts to the whole community from its constituent parts.

Decisions about what and how those narratives and ritual practices are to be presented involve negotiations among the constituencies of the congregations. This occurs in symbolic ways in the implicit expectations at Cedar Grove that the interdependence and interplay of black and white presence must be visible in the election of officers, those who usher, and among those who speak for the congregation in community events. It occurs in the deliberate expansion of narratives to include diverse cultural perspectives at Oakhurst and increasingly at Northwoods.

The effect of these decisions involves two possibilities in the way "students" make sense of what has been presented. For some, a teaching or practice is reproduced; that is, students select that which confirms or extends the received messages of an educational activity as if no discontinuity existed between past and present. For others, the same educational activity may lead to the rejection of the familiar and the appropriation of a language process or cultural pattern alien to their own cultural or religious tradition. Although learning often occurs along cultural, gender, or class lines, it is just as likely to cross those lines. A number of life-long "low church" Protestants at Northwoods, for example, have begun to adopt the practice of the pastor and a number of former Liberian Anglicans in making the sign of the cross when receiving the elements of the Lord's supper and at the conclusion of corporate prayers. Less tangible but perhaps more intriguing is the increasing ability of members in each congregation to participate in alien practices and processes, suspending for the time being their preference for certain language processes and cultural patterns. At Oakhurst people move back and forth between the meters of the Scottish psalter and the rhythms of the gospel choir. At Northwoods, African and European-American members wonder at their lack of offense during a Pentecost Sunday service when the Spanish-speaking pastor began to speak in tongues. What seems to be emerging in the educational practices of these congregations is the nurture of an appreciation of multiplicity that does not oppress or demean difference, but affirms the struggle involved in negotiating difference in creating those common events that nurture their common life.

Teaching and Learning: Communal Theologizing

One of the most difficult tasks we encountered in this study was to discern how these congregations ordered their lives for the "deliberate, systematic, and sustained" educational effort central to the task of forming a notion of community into which they might live with commitment and meaning. We quickly learned we had to look beyond the Sunday school. We also discovered quite quickly that each pastor assumed a clear and explicit role in teaching—especially through the leadership of worship, but in almost every other setting of the congregation as well. For Nibs and Caroline and Martha this role also extended into the community beyond the congregation.

We found in Alex Haley's description of the *griot*—the village wise man and storyteller in his ancestral village in Africa—an image for their role as teacher. This image began to illumine something of the way they contributed to the "primary socialization" of the people in these congregations into an emerging vision of Christian community. The *griot* sits at a central place in the village. In a similar fashion, when Jerome preaches from the table at the center of the Northwoods church, or Nibs gathers up the concerns of the congregation from the central aisle of Oakhurst, or all three stand or sit at the edge of some circle in congregational life, people are gathered into exchanges integral to the interplay of teaching and learning. Despite the linear pews at Oakhurst and Cedar Grove the dominant social structural image in each congregation begins in a circle that spirals out into the community.[24]

Each pastor, in quite different ways, instructs in didactic ways. Rev. Martha, in the middle of a sermon, will lean over the pulpit, look down at the congregation, and interrupt herself to announce, "I want all children to listen carefully now." Then she defines a word, puts it or some story into historical or theological perspective, or identifies an implication particularly relevant to their experience. Just as frequently Jerome will ask congregants to take up the bibles in the pew racks and to work through a passage of scripture verse by verse with him. A diligent student who begins his study of lectionary texts at 5:30 each morning, he describes the historical and social context for the passage, carries on a dialogue between that text and others his study has identified as filling out meanings to be found in the text as well as between the text and local, national, or global issues. Each Sunday morning while congregants are sharing their concerns for the week, Nibs will not only restate each concern so all can hear, but he describes its social context and pertinent theological and ethical implications. Similar interventions occur during prayer circles, pastoral visits, and in the flow of business meetings.

If we can carry forward the image of communities gathered around their pastors as the primary teacher, a second feature in the structure of these congregations as teaching-learning communities soon becomes apparent. It embodies the historic concerns of what has been called the teaching office of the church.[25] In these three congregations the office of teacher is both centralized and shared. The pastors in an informal but highly authoritative way gather others into the instructional role that gives order to congregational learning. At Cedar Grove the pattern is most flexible. It occurred as Rev. Martha found black and white lay leaders willing to assume the responsibility for exploring issues in some depth and to engaging others in the same process. This process does not occur in classrooms but when laity present a five-minute introduction to some issue in the community during worship and whenever and wherever people are engaged in conversation about some issue in the lives of church members or the larger community. In a sense, the structure of teaching spirals out into the congregation and community through whomever happens to be "delegated" at the moment to carry it. The settings for this next level of teaching are informal—in the conversations on the lawn, around fellowship meals, over the phone.

The authority for teaching at Oakhurst originates in the team ministry of Nibs and his ordained spouse, Caroline. It occurs not only through traditional roles of preaching and teaching. The Session of the church authorized Nibs to write to the city's newspapers to convey its perspectives on important justice issues in public life. It sanctioned a sabbatical leave so that he might write a book on the struggle with racism. Other members of the congregation are delegated to take up specific responsibilities in the spiraling expansion of the teaching circle—sometimes in a class setting but often in the implementation of some mission priority of the congregation. Some carry theological credentials into these responsibilities. Others carry the Oakhurst vision of a societal weaving that includes them and the people in the situation in which they find themselves. These places range from the work settings of the hospital kitchen, to ecumenical church meetings, to a grand jury courtroom. During the year of our study we observed the expansion of the inner circle of the Oakhurst teaching office to encompass an African-American laywoman whose ordination as an elder with primary responsibility for Christian education provided congregational affirmation for her partnership with Nibs and Caroline in the teaching ministry of the congregation.

At Northwoods the process had only begun to be shared. Jerome instituted a staff advisory committee, which included the youth minister, those leading the Spanish-speaking ministry, the director of music ministry, two members of the congregation with theological training, and students in the congregation from a nearby theological school. This group provided a community of reflection on congregational concerns. Each person brought concerns and perspectives from the congregation to illumine the group's conversation, which, in turn, significantly influenced each individual's leadership in the programs of the church.

The centrality of teaching in these congregations underscores the character of the patterns of corporate theological reflection. In his study of the teaching office of the church, Richard Osmer identifies three central tasks to this process. The first involves "the determination of the normative beliefs and practices of the church." None of these congregations has called into question its basic reformed or Wesleyan theological heritage, but each in its own way expresses considerable frustration with the dominant cultural perspectives of its larger church body in the articulation and transmission of those beliefs and practices. This frustration focuses much of the teaching agenda: to reinterpret "these beliefs and practices" for the radically shifting cultural and historical context they seek to create. Due to the diversity of theological perspectives, often rooted in cultural and class relationships, these pastors find themselves mediating viewpoints across the differences of congregational belief and practice all the time. That diversity of viewpoints engages them in the quest to interpret received texts and practices in ways that can be heard and responded to by their diverse constituencies. This occurs when Nibs sets in context the prayer requests of Oakhurst church members or takes time out in a Session meeting to review the background and perspectives on an issue under discussion. It happens at Cedar Grove when Rev. Martha asks people to listen carefully to what others are saying. It distinctively influences the preaching style of Jerome, who takes first one perspective on an issue or idea, then another, and yet another before developing some new insight for a life of discipleship in a pluralistic church and world. The result is heard in comments following the worship service: "That was a powerful sermon, but I still can't tell if he agrees with the Democrats or Republicans, with the liberals or conservatives—he seems to find some truth in each perspective."

A third task of the teaching office involves the formation and sustenance of educational institutions, processes, and curricula. It is at this point that we begin to see alternative patterns for education emerging in the lives of these three congregations. Self-consciously building on an old African proverb—It takes a whole village to raise a child—each congregation challenges the peer-segmented educational ministries in most U.S. Christian churches with explicit efforts to establish relationships among children, youth, and adults. Hence one of the most interesting moments in the Sunday schedule at Oakhurst occurs just prior to the worship service as Caroline and one or two other women pair off children from the community whose parents are not present with adults in the congregation. Children and youth enter freely into business meetings and adult conversations at Cedar Grove. The youth at Northwoods plan ways to get to know adults in the congregations on a personal level. In all three churches most children and youth are involved in the worship service and are almost omnipresent during fellowship meals, mission projects, and some workdays. Although each congregation continues to use purchased curriculum resources for classes and programs, the primary curriculum grows out of the liturgical, mission, and social life of the congregation. The intensity of intergenerational relationships reinforces the language, rituals, and values integral to congregational life for children and youth.

SUMMARY

The commitment to embrace diversity requires these three congregations to be about the continuing task of forming and reforming community. The presence of difference is both a destabilizing force and a resource for creativity and transformation. The focus on forming community centers the educative impulse in the primary events of congregational life—especially in weekly worship and the holy days of the church year. During times of intensified and sustained learning other programs and structures of the congregation provide an ecology of support to the experiences and meanings most closely associated with those events. The dynamics of teaching and learning contributing most clearly to the emerging visions of congregational identity and mission originate with the leadership of the pastors and key lay leaders and then spiral out through the life and work of the congregations. In that process children, youth, and adults are gathered into conversations in Sunday school, committee meetings, and social occasions, which, in predominantly informal ways, clarify meanings from their shared experiences and identify implications for their lives and for their congregations.

Notes

1. Lawrence A. Cremin, *American Education: The National Experience 1783-1876* (New York: Harper Colophon Books, 1982 [1980]), ix; see also Walter Brueggemann, *The Creative Word: Canon as a Model for Biblical Education* (Philadelphia: Fortress Press, 1982), 1.

2. C. A. Bowers, *Elements of a Post-Liberal Theory of Education* (New York: Teachers College Press, 1987), 137.

3. Most contemporary writings on education—including those which espouse a multicultural perspective—approach questions of the role of diversity in teaching and learning from within a dominant culture assumptive framework. Even religious educators (e.g., C. Ellis Nelson, John Westerhoff, Maria Harris) who emphasize communal dynamics in their theoretical writings give little attention to the dynamics of diversity in community. The challenge of maintaining attention to diversity may best be illustrated in the work of C. A. Bowers and David J. Flinders. In *Responsive Teaching: An Ecological Approach to Classroom Patterns of Language, Culture, and Thought* (New York: Teachers College Press, 1990), Bowers and Flinders develop a theoretical framework for teachers faced with an ecology of "cultural patterns and learning styles." In an essay in a more philosophical work Bowers explores the task of education as "the restoration of community" without clarifying the challenge that task presents to teachers and students in communities with an ecology of communal memories (*Elements of a Post-Liberal Theory of Education*, 137, 141).

4. John H. Westerhoff III, *Values for Tomorrow's Children: An Alternative Future for Education in the Church* (Philadelphia: Pilgrim Press, 1970), 58-59.

5. C. Ellis Nelson, *Where Faith Begins* (Richmond: John Knox Press, 1967), 10.

6. Robert W. Lynn, *Protestant Strategies of Education* (New York: Association Press, 1964).

7. In his study of nineteenth-century American U.S. education, Cremin observed that "the assumption of the dominant white community with respect to the Irish Catholics, the German Lutherans, and the Norwegian and Swedish Reformed was that they needed to be and could be Americanized—Americanization being a concept that was widely used to imply some combination of learning English, understanding the Constitution, living productively with the law according to middle-class standards, and accepting the values of an undenominational Protestant *paideia* . . . The prevailing assumption was clear: people could be educated to transcend barriers of ethnicity and religion in order to become full-fledged members of the American community, but they could not be educated to transcend the barriers of race" (*American Education*, 244-45).

8. For an introduction to the works of these educators, see Johann Heinrich Pestalozzi, *How Gertrude Teaches Her Children: An Attempt to Help Mothers Teach Their Own Children and an Account of the Method*, ed. Ebenezer Cooke, trans. Lucy E. Holland and Francis C. Turner (London: G. Allen and Unwin Ltd, 1915); Maria Montessori, *The Secret of Childhood*, trans. M. Joseph Costelloe (New York: Ballantine Books, 1973 [1966]); John Dewey, *Experience and Education* (New York: Collier Books, 1938); Jean Piaget, *The Development of Thought: Equilibration of Cognitive Structure*, trans. Arnold Rosin (New York: Viking Press, 1977); Erik H. Erikson, *Childhood and Society* (New York: Norton, 1962); Lawrence Kohlberg, *The Philosophy of Moral Development: Moral Stages and the Idea of Justice* (San Francisco: Harper & Row, 1981); James W. Fowler, *Stages of Faith: The Psychology of Human Development and the Quest for Meaning* (San Francisco: Harper & Row, 1981); Carol Gilligan, *In a Different Voice: Psychological Theory and Women's Development* (Cambridge: Harvard University Press, 1982).

9. For a recent critique of American U.S. schooling, see Jonathan Kozol, *Savage Inequalities: Children in America's Schools* (New York: Crown Publishers, Inc., 1991). Paulo Freire's now classic *Pedagogy of the Oppressed* established the agenda and analytical framework for a growing number of critical educational theorists. More recent representative voices and works include Michael W. Apple, *Ideology and Curriculum* (London: Routledge and Kegan Paul Ltd., 1979); Henry A. Giroux, *Schooling and the Struggle for Public Life: Critical Pedagogy in the Modern Age* (Minneapolis: University of Minnesota Press, 1988); Ira Shor, *Critical Teaching and Everyday Life* (Chicago: University of Chicago Press, 1980).

10. Freire, 70-1; Parker Palmer, *To Know As We Are Known: A Spirituality of Education* (San Francisco: Harper & Row, 1993), 69-75.

11. Mary Field Belenky, Blythe McVicker Clinchy, Nancy Rule Goldberger, and Jill Mattuck Tarule, *Women's Ways of Knowing: The Development of*

Self, Voice, and Mind (New York: Basic Books, 1986); Janice Hale, *Black Children: Their Roots, Culture, and Learning Styles* ((Provo, UT: Brigham Young University Press, 1982) and *Unbank the Fire: Visions for the Education of African American Children* (Baltimore: Johns Hopkins University Press, 1994); Gregory Cajete, *Look to the Mountain: An Ecology of Indigenous Education* (Durango, CO: Kivaki Press, 1994). Among the few who have begun to explore the dynamics of teaching and learning across cultural and gender boundaries are C. A. Bowers and David J. Flinders, *Responsive Teaching*; and bell hooks, *Teaching to Transgress: Education as the Practice of Freedom* (New York: Routledge, 1994).

12. Apple, 8.

13. hooks, 9, 11.

14. Harris, *Fashion Me a People: Curriculum in the Church* (San Francisco: Harper & Row, 1989), 42.

15. As we have already noted, interpreters of the voluntary nature of congregational life often emphasize the contribution of a principle of homogeneity in sustaining a congregation over time. At no point did we discover anyone describing a principle of heterogeneity in the discussion of voluntary societies, whether in congregations or other groups. We would note however, that in these congregations we do find an affirmation of the contributions of dissimilarity, of unlikeness, of significant, perhaps even incommensurable differences to their shared experience. Such a perspective on their common life, we suggest, contributes to a sense of anticipating the unexpected with as much intensity as most congregations exert to ensure their continuity as a communal reality into the future.

16. For a more detailed description of the nature of *event* as an organizing principle for congregational education, see C. Ellis Nelson, 87ff; and Charles R. Foster, *Educating Congregations: The Future of Christian Education* (Nashville: Abingdon Press, 1994), 37-50. Research into the educational practices of these three congregations helped to clarify the conceptual model developed in Foster.

17. Robert MacAfee Brown, *Is Faith Obsolete?* (Philadelphia: Westminster Press, 1974), 42-58.

18. Foster, 42-45.

19. One of the most provocative discussions on the role of imagination in teaching and learning may be found in Maria Harris, *Teaching and Religious Imagination* (San Francisco: Harper & Row, 1987), 16-22, 25-40.

20. R. S. Sugirtharajah, "Introduction," in *Voices from the Margins: Interpreting the Bible in the Third World*, ed. R. S. Sugirtharajah (Maryknoll, NY: Orbis Books, 1991), 1-2.

21. In a passionate essay Maxine Greene critiques traditional education with its concern for "initiating" students into the "'forms of life' R. S. Peters describes, or the public traditions, or the heritage" of a community or society. She notes that even when "emphasis has been placed on the importance of critical thinking or experimental intelligence, there has been a tendency to present an unexamined surface reality as 'natural,' fundamentally

unquestionable." In this tendency "to overlook the *constructed* character of social reality," education contributes to a "mystification" that "effectively obscures alienation" in the perceptions and experience of people. Greene calls for the creation "of the kinds of conditions that make possible a critique of what is taken to be 'natural,' of the 'forms of illusion' in which persons feel so 'completely at home,' no matter how alienated they are or how repressed." She encourages teachers and educators, in other words, to "combat mystification" for the sake of "a more authentic speaking" (*Landscapes of Learning* [New York: Teachers College Press, 1978], 54). Lawrence Grossberg included the quotation by David Bailey and Stuart Hall in "Introduction: Bringin' It All Back Home—Pedagogy and Cultural Studies," in *Between Borders: Pedagogy and the Politics of Cultural Studies*, ed. Henry A. Giroux and Peter McClaren (New York: Routledge, 1994), 14.

22. Bowers and Flinders, 2-3.

23. Bowers, *Elements of a Post-Liberal Theory of Education*, 147.

24. Alex Haley, *Roots: The Saga of an American Family* (New York: Dell Publishing, 1976), 716ff. Letty M. Russell explores this circular image of church in *Church in the Round*. This image encompasses the actions integral to gathering around the table and to moving back and forth from center to margins of church life as new people are welcomed and as members struggle to remain on the margins with the oppressed. In this search for "inclusive solidarity among different nationalities, classes, races, gender, and so much more," the church is built up "literally" by "going in circles" (*Church in the Round: Feminist Interpretation of the Church* [Louisville: Westminster/John Knox Press, 1993], 64). The dynamic character of seeing the church in the round is expanded by the ripple of the words and actions of the church into the larger community. The dynamics of teaching and learning in these congregations may be seen most clearly in these movements.

25. For a helpful discussion of the teaching office see Richard Robert Osmer, *A Teachable Spirit: Recovering the Teaching Office in the Church* (Louisville: Westminster/John Knox Press, 1990). He notes the church has emphasized three primary tasks: "1) the determination of the normative beliefs and practices of the church, 2) the reinterpretation of these beliefs and practices in shifting cultural and historical contexts, and 3) the formation and sustenance of educational institutions, processes and curricula by which the church's normative beliefs and practices are taught" (15).

7

CHANGE AND AMBIGUITY

New Practices of Faith and Knowing

> We're a changing church! Of course we're changing! Shouldn't every church be always changing? I mean . . . but, maybe we're not going somewhere—or, what was the word?—"in transition"—we're just a changing church.
>
> —A European-American woman at Cedar Grove

INTRODUCTION

Some sixty Cedar Grove Church members had gathered after a covered-dish supper to hear our preliminary findings following our year of research in their congregation. We had just stated that in many cases denominational officials see churches like theirs as *transitional* churches destined to become *black* after having been *white*. The woman quoted above was approximately fifty or more years old and had been a member of the church her whole life. Her sense of the church as continuously dynamic struck us as profound.

As we have already observed, one of the noteworthy characteristics of all three congregations in this study is their strikingly high tolerance of change and ambiguity. They are often not clear about the "proper" way of carrying out their tasks, and they are often very aware of not knowing where they are *going*. Indeed, they sometimes seem to have the sense that perhaps they are not *going* somewhere but are *being* a dynamic church. They are not seeking to *resolve* but rather to *embrace* and *live faithfully* in the ambiguity and change that seems to them characteristic of life and of who they are as a church.

We suggest in this chapter that the ways in which persons in these culturally diverse congregations accept, embrace, celebrate, and participate in the ambiguity and change of their own communities 1) prepares them to participate well in and work toward the transformation of the larger society in which they live; and 2) predisposes them to understand society and their world in distinctively pluralistic terms. Put another way, the diversity within these communities prepares members to be effective and sophisticated in their participation in the wider society that is similarly struggling with issues of diversity and difference. It also precipitates a form of consciousness different from the norm in most homogenous communities. This form of consciousness may be characterized as *pluralistic*. We will explore aspects of this form of consciousness in terms of epistemology, hermeneutics, and faith—the infrastructure for the dynamics of discerning meaning central to the tasks of forming, maintaining, and renewing community.

MULTILINGUALITY INSIDE AND OUT

In a characteristically insightful and influential interpretation of 2 Kings 18-19, Walter Brueggemann argues that Christians must be *bilingual*—conversant "in the communal language of their own tradition" as well as the public language of the secular realm.[1] Brueggemann uses the imagery of the wall from 2 Kings (in which the Assyrians are at Judah's city wall), to create a metaphor for these two languages—the conversation "at the wall" and the conversation "behind the wall." Brueggemann contends that good citizenship and good discipleship require effective participation in these two different conversations wherein two different hermeneutics must be used: a sectarian hermeneutic *behind* the wall, which assumes the reality of "the rigorous norms" of YHWH; and a public hermeneutic *at* the wall, which is suspicious of but nonetheless engages the public language (in which YHWH's reality is not assumed). Furthermore, according to Brueggemann, the discourse behind the wall strengthens and prepares one (the Israelites . . . us) for participation with openness and integrity at the wall.

This scheme helpfully illumines ways in which the congregations of this study are conscious of being alternative communities to the dominant culture—of operating out of a "different practice of perception, epistemology, and language" and holding "to a set of alternative values."[2] This notion of bilinguality also illumines ways in which these congregations nonetheless engage the dominant culture in the culture's own language by being responsible citizens and disciples, living their sectarian visions publicly.

But these congregations and their sectarian hermeneutics are distinctly unlike the Israel of 2 Kings. These communities are characteristically diverse. Pluralism exists not just at their walls but also behind the walls. The "different practice of perception, epistemology, and language" behind these walls is not just a different set of perceptions. It is not just that different things are known, or even that different realities pertain. Rather, different ways of perceiving, knowing, and speaking become operative. That is to say, different *practices* of perception, epistemology, and language are at play—different from Israel behind the wall, and different from the Israel-Assyria confrontation at the wall; that is, different from the practices of "like-minded" or "like-kinded" communities and different from the dominant practices of society at large. This practice does not grow out of the assumed realities of a stable community identity (as in the case of Israel behind the wall). It is a practice based in the multiple realities of a conversation with multiple, diverse, and changing participants similar to conversations at the wall, *except that the conversations of these congregations form a community rather than a confrontation.* In other words, the public and sectarian conversational *practices* of these congregations are not so different from each other as Brueggemann's scheme might lead us to expect. These congregations are public churches. They engage a public hermeneutic, a hermeneutic of multiplicity, negotiation, and change, both within and beyond their walls. They are not just bilingual—speaking one language in the sect and one in public—but are multilingual and multicultural both in their communal and in their public conversations and relations.

It may be argued that we are all multilingual in the metaphoric sense in which we are using the term here. Anyone who manages to communicate publicly does so by speaking and understanding more than the private language of some specific group. But the point here is that in these communities irreducible multipleness and ongoing multiplication (of languages, cultures, differences) become part of their self-understanding and part of their basic perceptions of how things are. This is not a traditional modern way of perceiving self and world, although it may be a part of an emerging *postmodern* practice of perception.[3]

Multilinguality is explicit and literal at Northwoods Church. For many members a shift in the congregation's perception of itself first occurred when one of the first Hispanic members sang a solo in Spanish during worship. "It was beautiful, not an eye was dry" reported numerous European-American members who cannot understand more than a few words in Spanish. Another high point in this congregation's worship life occurred on Pentecost Sunday. In a dramatization of the first Pentecost, youth prayed simultaneously in six or seven native languages from the center dais during worship. Congregants reported that "it was like the first Pentecost." "Each heard in their own language." "You could feel the presence of the Spirit."

Bilinguality or multilinguality is required of these Christians not just so they can participate in the conversation at the wall but so they can participate in their own communal conversation. But, as in the case of this particular congregation, very few people are genuinely bilingual, and no one is sufficiently multilingual to claim mastery of all the languages present within the community, much less within the society. The task persons in these communities face is *not* that of becoming bilingual or multilingual or multicultural in the sense of mastering the multiple languages and cultures in currency. Rather, their task is to *appreciate* and *live in* rather than *master* or *resolve* the multiplicity of languages and cultures among them. Life in these communities calls persons toward the perception that experience can and should be interpreted and named in various ways, that truth can and should be viewed from differing angles simultaneously. Robert Kegan speaks of such conscious appreciation and acceptance of multiplicity as "a new form of consciousness" emerging to meet the particular demands of contemporary life.[4] James Fowler observes that such a way of perceiving is among the prominent characteristics of "conjunctive faith."[5] The experience of the participants in these three congregations suggests that persons and communities that embrace diversity are called to such consciousness and to such faith perspectives.

The call to appreciation and acceptance can be heard in Rev. Martha's repeated phrase at Cedar Grove Church that some particular person or cultural group is "just like that, and they're not going to change." The phrase is meant to point to the cultural basis of some idiosyncratic behavior; the implication is "you may never, and do not need to, *understand* it . . . but you do need to accept them and live with them as brother and sister just the same." A similar dynamic can be seen in the willingness of some Oakhurst members to "go ahead and inadvertently offend people, and then patch things up later," because seeking sufficient prior mastery of the other's culture in order to avoid inadvertent offense would mean never being ready to speak. Being multilingual or multicultural here does not mean mastering but rather embracing multiple meanings.

Seeking to live in the multiplicity of languages and cultures rather than to master them—to live with rather than to resolve ambiguity—points to a distinctive way of being in community. Embracing multiplicity and ambiguity in community implies that communal identity is not based on a shared language or common culture. Rather, a shared imagination seems to animate and sustain these communities. At Northwoods the constant imagery of Revelation 7—"all the nations and tribes shall gather together before the throne of God"—enlivens the members' image of themselves. At Oakhurst the imagery of Ephesians 2—depicting Christ as the one who "breaks down the dividing walls of hostility"—animates ways they talk about their congregational mission. At Cedar Grove Church the image of the church as "family" binding together descendants of Africa and Europe in the mutuality of caring familial relations (for better and for worse) characterizes the congregation's vision. And all of these visions inform, or "fund," a distinctive "counter-imagination," as Brueggemann puts it—a vision of the way things *might be* in the face of a culture and an immediate context where things are *not* this way.[6] Racial tensions do exist in the society and in the neighborhoods of these churches and continue occasionally to disrupt these congregations. Cultural differences do create impediments to communication and to community building. But their "counter-imaginations" continually see beyond what is and help create what might be.

The capacity of members of these congregations to live with and embrace a multiplicity of languages and cultures points to a particular sort of faith. It is a faith without the certainty of uniformity and sameness. It is a faith that does not rely on what is, but lives instead with multiple possibilities and imagines what might be. This is not an easy faith. As Sharon Welch has written,

> The courage to act and think within an uncertain framework is not easily achieved. It may be that this is what is meant by faith. Faith is not belief. . . . It is a stance of being, an acceptance of risk and openness, an affirmation of both the importance of life

(its dimension of ultimate significance) and the refusal to collapse that ultimacy into a static given, identifying it as defini-
tively achieved in some concrete medium of its manifestation.[7]

In some sense this faith without certainty was forced upon members of these congregations. In each case rapid and dramatic demographic changes in their neighborhoods created the uncertain
framework for congregational life and mission. And in each case
those who decided to stay found themselves faced not only with the
uncertainty of declining membership and changing demographics in
the larger communities in which they are located, but also the uncertainty of being continually engaged in the processes of forming and
re-forming community. Yet in another sense this faith emerged from
the decision to stay and live into the new possibilities of their changing situations.

Uncertainty runs deep in these communities. The Presbytery urged
Oakhurst Church at least twice to close its doors; a professional
researcher predicted that Northwoods Church would be forced to
do so by now; and many of Cedar Grove's conference officials over
the past fifteen years have wanted it to quit playing at being "in
transition" and become a black church.

Uncertainty characterizes these communities in a myriad of more
subtle ways. The norms in diverse communities are continuously up
for grabs. What is "good" music? What is "proper" attire, or "cour-
teous" behavior, or "normal" breakfast food, or "*traditional*" Christian beliefs or practices? None of these are well established in these
communities; multiple views keep them in constant negotiation. That
process can take a long time. Northwoods leaders, for example, have
discovered that if a congregational event is to be considered a suc-
cess by its various constituencies, it must be planned, approved, and
participated in by persons from as many cultural groups as possible.
At times Oakhurst members say, with discomfort in their voices,
"We really don't know what we are doing." At other times they say
with an expectant smile, "You never know quite what is going to
happen here." These congregations, in other words, experience ambiguity and uncertainty as both threat and promise.

EPISTEMOLOGY: KNOWING AND PRODUCING
KNOWLEDGE IN CONTEXTS OF DIVERSITY

Insofar as communities can be seen as producers of knowledge
and faith,[8] the ways these diverse communities go about producing

their knowledge and their faith, and the subsequent character of that knowledge and that faith, are different from those of more homogenous communities. The experience of being constantly confronted with difference and needing to negotiate a provisional consensus may bring toward consciousness the constructed and political nature of traditions, assumptions and values, truth, and knowledge. We say *toward* consciousness because it is unlikely that many people in these congregations would speak of knowledge as socially constructed or of knowledge as power in the theoretical way that some academicians do.[9] Indeed they do not tend to speak at all of knowledge in the theoretical way that we are using the term here. Yet they do speak of ways in which the dominant truth or reality over against which their community stands is distorted and/ or serves oppressive and unjust political purposes. We introduce theoretical reflection on ways people in these congregations seem to form and view knowledge because epistemology (one's ways of approaching and understanding knowledge) and faith (one's ways of approaching and understanding the deep meanings of life) are closely related.

For each of these congregations, the first steps toward becoming a culturally diverse congregation were characterized by struggles to embrace the racial diversity given to them in their contexts rather than seeing it as a problem or tension to be resolved. Their growing consciousness of legitimate racial diversity, however, then seemed to evoke increasing awareness of gender, age, sexual orientation,[10] social class, and country or region of origin as diversities also to be lived in, embraced, and celebrated.

This experience of proliferating diversities impinges upon epistemology. If a person perceives the need to embrace diverse others and to participate with them in the process of constructing working understandings of the world, and if these diverse others continue to multiply, it may begin to appear that this process of constructing knowledge (or working understandings of the world) is continually at play and is always provisional. The recognition of diversity and the presumption of change and ambiguity become part of a basic orientation to life, a basic way of understanding the world. There is cultural and socioeconomic diversity, political and theological diversity, regional and linguistic diversities within cultural groups; indeed there are diversities in musical preference, worship style, personality type, and on and on. How does one negotiate the dynamics of shared community life respectfully and responsibly in the midst all this diversity? How does one gather everyone into the dynamics of making decisions? How can one know what is true and right and good if multiple perspectives are present and respected at every turn?

Each of these three congregations has evolved a common (although long) process for reaching decisions. Dozens of people discuss decisions in numerous informal contexts at Cedar Grove Church before they come to the floor of an official meeting, and even then it is not uncommon for an issue to be broached at two or three meetings before coming to a vote. At Oakhurst ideas and decisions must be run through an extensive series of formalized channels. And at Northwoods congregational leaders have become increasingly sensitive to the necessity of employing different strategies for building consensus or moving beyond consensus to encouraging involvement of diverse national cultural groups in church events.

Northwoods discovered the limits to traditional Eurocentric and middle-class patterns of decision-making while developing a new mission statement. The process began in a retreat of the Administrative Council. An extra effort was made to ensure the presence of new council members from other countries—to ensure their representation (a majority-minority power strategy). This group went through a fairly typical brainstorming process to identify and set priorities for major themes for the statement. The chairwoman appointed a task force of four persons, women with European-American, Liberian, and Jamaican backgrounds and a European-American man—all relative newcomers—to write a statement to be presented to the next Administrative Council meeting. Although it was probably not her intent, their inclusion did not mean they shared fully in the power structure of the congregation. Long-time members still had enough votes to modify, ratify, or reject their work if they should choose to do so. The council spent another two meetings refining the committee's report. In United Methodist majority-minority polity procedures, the council could then adopt the statement or recommend it to the annual meeting of the church. Discussion in the council about the lack of input of many different voices in the congregation, however, altered this process. The council concurred that, while the statement was produced by a representative body, it did not yet reflect the thinking of the whole congregation. Consequently, the proposed statement was printed in the newsletter and read during two worship services. Paper and pencils were provided for comments. Each of the youth and adult Sunday school classes spent a session working through the statement, identifying ways to critique and strengthen it. Since most of the international members of the congregation did not belong to the adult classes, some members of the council agreed to contact these persons individually to obtain their reactions and suggestions. These comments were given to the task force, which once again worked on the statement before presenting it to the council. This revised statement went through the same process, this time with few new suggestions. So the council approved it, acknowledging that new circumstances would probably require changes in the future. In this effort the congregation moved beyond the political negotiations of majority rule through the compromises integral to a strategy of consensus, to the development of a statement built out of the contributions of all participants. The process was not easy. It took a long time. It generated strong argument. It required intense listening. It evoked considerable laughter. And it intensified shared awareness of differences in perspectives and practices among church members.

Awareness of differences within these congregations may heighten their awareness of other differences in the community and society around them. Evidence of such a broadening awareness of difference may be seen in Oakhurst's effort to bring gay and lesbian voices into their community discourse. It may be at work in the attempts at Northwoods to recruit Vietnamese persons into the congregation (none were currently present). The enthusiasm for difference in these efforts contributes to the celebration of a broad vision that an appreciative consciousness of diversity creates. This consciousness contributes to a more holistic view of the experience of human life in the world and of one's own place in that world. Many members of these congregations say they come explicitly for the diversity. They value a place where they can experience "others" as peers and siblings in a spiritual community. This experience broadens their knowledge of themselves and others, and may transform their understandings and practices of knowledge and knowing.

A HERMENEUTIC OF MULTIPLICITY AND CHANGE

Hermeneutic refers to the lens or perspective or set of assumptions through which experience is processed, or through which life is "read." The members of these culturally diverse congregations increasingly seem to understand life as characterized by multiplicity and change. They see everything as a slice of the multiplicity of things and as a moment in the ongoing process of life changes. "Our life has known the movement of the city" reads Oakhurst's mission statement:

> We were once all of a kind. Then our church became multira-
> cial. . . . And our people were afraid, afraid of ourselves from
> different races, afraid of ourselves from different cultures. The
> faithfulness of those who stayed and those who came gave us
> courage. By God's power we have been given grace through
> what we thought was our weakness. In the midst of our fears
> God has surprised us and blessed us. The diversity which we
> feared has empowered us to confront God's truth in the world.

As this statement infers, the awareness of multiplicity was essentially forced on some members. Those early members who "were
once all of a kind" initially responded with fear as their community
and "world" changed from being racially and culturally homogeneous to being diverse, from appearing singular to appearing multiple. This consciousness of multiplicity was also forced upon some
other members. Those new African-American members, by virtue of
their minority status in the society and in the church, were and are
confronted by a dominant culture that defines them as "different"
or "other." They know there is difference, otherness, multipleness
because they do not fit the assumed norms of the dominant culture.
For these people comfort could be and often is sought in the experience of being a part of and the "same" as a "like-kinded" community—a black church, an African-American (or Asian, or Hispanic, or
other) neighborhood, a majority black school. These members too
experienced fear as they became part of a multiracial community.

But as the mission statement (written by a biracial lay task force,
and later approved by the Session and congregation) also suggests,
the experience of multiplicity became transformative. "In the midst
of our fears God has surprised us and blessed us." Part of what has
been transformed is their basic understanding of how the church
and the world ought to be. Members often told us that "this is what
the church ought to be about" and "this is how life really is." They
see themselves as a microcosm, and as they look out they see diversity, multiplicity, and change everywhere. And they see this as a blessing rather than a curse—"the diversity which we feared has
empowered us." "We are a changing church! (and that is our blessing and strength!)"

Church members seem increasingly to read life through such lenses.
Yet they understand that many still fear multiplicity and change, just
as at times a new experience of difference confronts them with their
own predilections to fear. When the Outreach committee at
Northwoods went door to door throughout the neighborhood to

invite people to church, the courage and hopefulness that propelled them were challenged. At a number of doors no English was spoken; at many others communication felt strained and fragmentary at best. They experienced fear and discouragement. But they had expected to face cultural barriers (they were coming to see multipleness and diversity in the world and to read their experiences through these lenses). Their mission was and is to negotiate those barriers so as to invite everyone to the table of fellowship and thus move toward the realization of the eschatological image of the multiplicity of humankind in one communion (or the shattering of dividing walls at Oakhurst, or the all-inclusive family at Cedar Grove). This sacramental image of everyone being present at the table of fellowship is glimpsed at Northwoods when they gather around the communion rail at the center of their octagonal sanctuary for the Lord's Supper or to join hands and pray together at the end of a worship service. Oakhurst's image of the shattering of walls is glimpsed when they openly share personal joys and concerns in the middle of their worship service. At Cedar Grove the image of the all-inclusive family is glimpsed at family night suppers and informal gatherings after worship.

Yet even though hopeful visions are regularly glimpsed, even though they may feel themselves moving toward the realization of their visions, a sense of fear and weariness is never far away. When a Haitian family visited Northwoods one Sunday, the pastor welcomed them, but he also found himself silently bewailing the implications of their presence. If they returned, he would have to be as attentive to Haiti in his preaching, teaching, and praying as he had been to Somalia, Korea, Liberia, and other ancestral homes of church members. The issue was not Haiti, but the burden of further expanding his attention. These experiences of multiplying diversities point up the burdens of operating with a hermeneutic of multiplicity and change rather than a hermeneutic of sameness and assimilation. The naiveté that underlies so much liberal rhetoric of inclusion fades away under the weight of these burdens, as leaders and members of these congregations undertake the hard work of negotiating a community of diversity.

Their experience with difference, the negotiation of barriers, and the acceptance of the burdens of openness within the church empowers them to reach out toward diverse others and to participate in the complex and changing society in which they live. Members of these churches are actively involved in local city government. They serve on school boards and civic councils. They understand civic life as complex and multiform; they do not expect to master or determine or direct it. But they do feel the responsibility and the ability to *participate* in shaping it. Society is a system of which they are a part and which they help to shape and define—a system not unlike their own Christian communities, a system whose complexity, multifariousness, and messiness they choose to live in.

This eagerness to participate in the multiplicity and complexity and even messiness of life can be heard in a passing remark made by Nibs Stroupe. We had brought a group of consultants to visit Oakhurst. After showing us a room recently converted from a clothes closet to a classroom he concluded: "It's a little messy, but that's all right. We like to keep things messy around here—it reminds us that life is never really neat and clean the way you might want it." Indeed they *like* to keep things a little messy, because that's "how life really is." When they see something too neat and too clean, they become suspicious that someone is hiding the messiness—forcing uniformity on the complex multiplicity of life, forcing out of view the challengingly diverse "others"; or proclaiming a moment in human time (a snapshot of an apparently clean room) as the general character of human life. One might speak of a "hermeneutic of suspicion" here, and that might be useful. But the assumption underlying the suspicion is that there is a human tendency to fear and avoid the multiple, complex, and messy nature of life.

FAITH FORMATION IN DIVERSE COMMUNITIES

We have been discussing and relating epistemology, hermeneutics, and faith. *Faith* may be understood to be one's basic orientation in life; it identifies life's ultimate character and meaning. *Epistemology* refers to one's ways of knowing—of comprehending, making sense, and creating meaning. Following people like Brueggemann and Ricoeur, we have taken *hermeneutics* beyond textual interpretation to refer to one's means or ways of interpreting and construing the meaning of experience.[11] These three—epistemology, faith, and hermeneutics—do not seem so different from one another. Or perhaps they are all "of a part." Perhaps they are each a part of what some mean by "consciousness."[12] Perhaps they are not each a *part* of a whole but are varying forms of expression for the multifarious whole itself—one's global understanding of and orientation toward life, which in turn determines one's interpretive lenses and identifying commitments.

In any case, the question to be asked now is not just, What is the character of the faith in these communities and how is that faith formed? It is, rather, What (presuming that faith is integral to what we have been addressing all along) contributes to the emergence of the orientation to the world, the way of knowing, the way of interpreting experience which these congregations have come to value and thrive on?

Part of the answer to this question can be stated rather simply: An experience of grace in the presence of change and multiplicity leads toward this faith. But this experience is not easily understood. Perhaps it is something like the "faith of loss" that Robert Bellah describes—a relinquishing of some familiar, understandable, and previously treasured knowledge or meanings or assumptions, and a discovery that the world does not then fall apart but is somehow even more deeply meaningful than before.[13]

Perhaps the experience of diversity within a caring community precipitates movement toward what James Fowler calls "conjunctive faith"; that is, "a felt sense that truth is . . . multiform and complex" and must "in its richness, ambiguity, and multi-dimensionality . . . be approached from at least two or more angles of vision simultaneously."[14] Fowler's discussion centers on the faith of adults. The conjunctive-like faith associated with experiences of diversity, however, is not just for adults. Children participate in and identify with the meanings of this faith that embraces change and multiplicity because they help form and live out of the communal ethos in which they are located.

Perhaps these congregations embrace something like the self-consciously "constructive faith" of which Gordon Kaufman writes—wherein faith is lived "in face of the ultimate mystery of life" but with joy for the "serendipitous creativity of the universe," in which God, and we, and all else participate.[15] But how does this happen? How does such faith arise for these people? How do they, or how might they, intentionally sponsor the formation of such faith?

When asked how they came to have the vision they presently have of church and of life as multiple and changing and therefore good, nearly all responded by describing transformative experiences of the "other": missionary experiences in Africa years ago; a few weeks spent in New York City as a teen-age southerner; a confusingly close yet distanced relationship to a black nanny as a white child; a black man's experience of being befriended by a white teen-age boy; an elderly convalescing white man being visited by a group of African, Caribbean, Hispanic, and European-American youth; a group of

European-American and African-American men supervising a barbecue pit together through the night; a black family being visited by
a remarkably earnest white woman pastor; and on and on their stories go. The point is that these experiences of intimacy or identification with an "other" underwrite the faith these people find themselves
living into. Being in relationship to new and *different* people in new
and different ways precipitates the possibility of living faithfully in
the midst of the change and ambiguity that emerges out of their
growing awareness of each other. These relational experiences fund
their imaginations and sponsor images for their communal life.

In a sense this suggests that social conditions that allow for or set
up a context for mutual communication among persons are prereq-
uisite to ethical and transformative relationships.[16] People need to
do things together in order to communicate and to have their knowledge transformed. This is not an abstract concept to the people at
Oakhurst and Cedar Grove. On numerous occasions when we asked
different people why they got along so well across racial and cultural lines, we heard some variation on "because we work together."
But they also reminded us in a variety of ways that their life together
is messy as well. What arises out of their interrelational experiences
is often not some new clear insight or understanding, but a subtle
shift in practices of perception, epistemology, and language concern-
ing what is—and an awakening of imagination as to what might be.
This imagination may then be further funded by biblical texts that
illumine or support it or that themselves offer alternative hopeful
realities.[17]

In effect, this is the general pedagogical approach of these congregations. They work to create contexts where people can experience each other, engage in the mutuality of some shared project, and
proclaim texts that envision an alternative reality or an alternative
future. They revel in covered-dish suppers, church maintenance
projects, and the formation of a cheering section at a high school
football game. They also engage in worship with energy and enthusiasm as a time for the proclamation of biblical images and for relating to and experiencing one another in the ritual structures of
communal intimacy and through rituals of greeting (often for ten
minutes or more during the worship service and more later) and
caring (through extensive announcements about the well-being of
those who are sick or have some special need and through interces-
sory prayer).

Perhaps this imaginative faith, which is comfortable with ambiguity and multiplicity, can be seen in the surprising energy and open-

endedness in Oakhurst's carefully planned but largely impromptu Christmas pageant, in which all persons present participate. Perhaps the surprise some members at Northwoods experienced when they realized they were *not surprised* when someone began speaking in tongues during a Pentecost worship service[18] illustrates something of this type of faith. Perhaps the image of Rev. Martha and some African-American teen-age girls spontaneously dancing to Polynesian rhythms played on a ukulele at a covered-dish supper is a metaphor for this imaginative faith and its formation. The ukulele was played by an active Roman Catholic layman of Hawaiian ancestry who plays volleyball at Cedar Grove Church. He assumed he would be welcome to a congregational dinner because Cedar Grove is "my family too." He brought his ukulele on a whim and decided to play for the fun of it during clean-up time, without asking permission. The girls joined in the dancing at Martha's urging. A small crowd gathered to watch and cheer before they continued the business at hand—to clean up after the dinner, to prepare for the program to follow, and to further the conversations that sustain their relationships with each other and revitalize their sense of identity and mission.

SUMMARY

The congregations of this study share a propensity to embrace not only diversity but also ambiguity and change. Indeed, we have suggested that a particular form of consciousness may emerge in communities and persons that celebrate diversity. This consciousness is characterized by an understanding of multiplicity and change as integral to life. Members of these congregations become "multilingual" and multicultural both in their intra-communal relations and in their relations to the larger society. They come to understand and interpret all experience through a lens of multiplicity and change—a consciousness of pluralism and dynamism.

This consciousness of pluralism and dynamism is embodied both in individuals and in the community and can be seen as shaping distinctive practices of knowledge, perception, and meaning—of epistemology, hermeneutics, and faith. In terms of epistemology, we see in these congregations an implicit awareness of the constructed and political nature of traditions, assumptions, values, truth, and knowledge. Their encounters with each other bring to awareness multiple culturally constructed perspectives on everything from breakfast foods to traditional Christian beliefs. They are continuously confronted with the necessity to negotiate some shared provisional understandings and to live with multiple immanent possibilities.

In terms of hermeneutics, members of these congregations tend to understand and interpret experience through a consciousness of multiplicity and change. They sense life to be more multiple than uniform, more dynamic than static, more messy than neat. When encountering difference, they tend to "read" the experience from this perspective. They increasingly look upon differences as part of the beauty of life. When faced with the appearance of sameness, many have begun to be suspicious that some important parts of the picture are being hidden.

The normative faith of these congregations may be spoken of as "conjunctive," "constructive," or as a willingness to live into and beyond "loss." Members of these congregations tend to be open to living into rather than resolving the ongoing changes and continuous ambiguities that characterize their life together. They seem to be living toward an emerging shared vision of who and what God has called them to become. In each congregation an often articulated vision of an alternative reality (humanity as a multiracial/multicultural family, an end to dividing walls of hostility, all the world gathered together at the table of fellowship) feeds and funds their imaginations and their faith.

The impetus to such faith, and the form of consciousness to which it is related, may be found in members' experiences of new relationships with diverse others. The nurturing of such relationships becomes central to the tasks of forming, maintaining, and renewing diverse communities of faith.

Notes

1. Walter Brueggemann, "The Legitimacy of a Sectarian Hermeneutic: 2 Kings 18-19," in Mary Boys, ed., *Education for Citizenship and Discipleship* (New York: Pilgrim Press, 1989), 4, 23, 9.

2. Ibid., p. 9.

3. Kenneth Gergen, for example, documents in *The Saturated Self*, the multiplication of self identities, or the "population of the self" as one primary dimension of contemporary postmodern consciousness (*The Saturated Self: Dilemmas of Identity in Contemporary Life* [New York: Basic Books, 1991]).

4. Robert Kegan, *In Over Our Heads: The Mental Demands of Modern Life* (Cambridge: Harvard University Press, 1994).

5. James W. Fowler, *Stages of Faith: The Psychology of Human Development and the Quest for Meaning* (San Francisco: Harper & Row, 1981), 185.

6. We are borrowing here from the language of Walter Brueggemann in *Texts Under Negotiation: The Bible and Postmodern Imagination* (Minneapolis: Fortress Press, 1993). This theme will be revisited later in this chapter.

7. Sharon Welch, *Communities of Resistance and Solidarity: A Feminist Theology of Liberation* (Maryknoll, NY: Orbis Books, 1985), 78.

8. The literature that argues for or assumes the "social construction" of knowledge and/or faith is extensive. Notable representatives are Peter L. Berger and Thomas Luckmann, *The Social Construction of Reality: A Treatise in the Sociology of Knowledge* (Garden City, NY: Doubleday, 1966); H. Richard Niebuhr, *The Meaning of Revelation*, (New York: Macmillan, 1960); Michel Foucault, *Power/Knowledge: Selected Interviews and Other Writings, 1972-1977*, ed. Colin Gordon (New York: Pantheon Books, 1980); Robert Schreiter, *Constructing Local Theologies* (Maryknoll, NY: Orbis Books, 1986); Iris Marion Young, *Justice and the Politics of Difference* (Princeton: Princeton University Press, 1990); Nancy Fraser, *Unruly Practices: Power, Discourse and Gender in Contemporary Social Theory* (Minneapolis: University of Minnesota Press, 1989); bell hooks, *Yearning: Race, Gender, and Cultural Politics* (Boston: South End Press, 1990).

9. We have been influenced in the ways we speak of the social construction and power dynamics of knowledge by theorists such as those listed in the previous note.

10. Homosexuality is overtly embraced and celebrated only at Oakhurst Church, where gay and lesbian rights are defended publicly and gay and lesbian persons are intentionally sought for membership. Homosexual persons have been warmly accepted as part of the other two congregations, but gays and lesbians are not publicly recognized, defended, or courted as such.

11. Brueggemann, "The Legitimacy of a Sectarian Hermeneutics"; Paul Ricoeur, *Hermeneutics and the Human Sciences: Essays on Language, Action, and Interpretation*, ed. and trans. John B. Thompson (Cambridge: Cambridge University Press, 1981).

12. E.g. Kegan, 6-8.

13. Robert N. Bellah, *Beyond Belief: Essays on Religion in a Post-Traditional World* (New York: Harper & Row, 1970), xix-xxi.

14. Fowler, p. 65. Other evidence of "conjunctive-like" faith can also be found in these congregations. Consider, for example, the intimations of a second naivete, and the ambiguous "conjunction" of particularity and openness in Oakhurst's labeling itself "multi-racial, forward-thinking, biblically-based, Jesus-centered."

15. Gordon D. Kaufman, *In Face of Mystery: A Constructive Theology* (Cambridge: Harvard University Press, 1993), 264ff.

16. Sharon D. Welch makes a similar point in *A Feminist Ethic of Risk* (Minneapolis: Fortress Press, 1990), 131.

17. Cf. Brueggemann, *Texts Under Negotiation*.

18. Speaking in tongues would, however, have become an issue to be addressed if it had happened more than once. There is a difference between a *surprise* and a *practice*.

8

LINGERING
REFLECTIONS

In the course of researching and writing this book some of our preliminary assumptions have been confirmed. Congregations that embrace diversity are intriguing instances of new ways of being community in contemporary society. A research methodology for gathering and interpreting data did emerge from our conversations with church members and leaders. Our own cultural and racial identities had to be negotiated in our relationship to the people in these congregations and in the development of our research methods.

We also discovered new insights. One of the most intriguing centered on our perception of the simultaneous fragility and vibrancy we experienced in and through these congregations. When one of the original congregations in the study decided to withdraw after less than one month, we respected but regretted that decision. After living with these three congregations for a year, we now have more appreciation for the sense of vulnerability its leaders may have been feeling at the time. In chapter 7 we explored the strengths and promises in the ways these congregations embrace change and ambiguity. We now recognize more fully that communities embracing change and ambiguity are not stable by definition. The possibility of dramatic, perhaps tragic change is always within sight. We are aware, for example, of other culturally diverse congregations where a new pastor, a shift in lay leadership, or some new demographic change shattered decisions to engage in ministries lived out of a praxis of multiplicity. Each of the congregations in this study experienced the possibility of radical change as threat—even to the threat of not surviving—at one time or another.

During the year of our research we became increasingly conscious of ways our questions contributed to their sense of fragility. Some questions—often dealing with matters of race, gender, culture, or power—brought into the open latent issues and concerns that then had to be addressed. We found ourselves worrying about the impact of our research. When we voiced our concern, church members usually told us to stop worrying. In a variety of ways, they said we had to take them as they are. In such moments members of these congregations reflected a boldly prophetic and stubbornly self-confirming view of the vitality of their common life. Cedar Grove and Oakhurst clearly thought they provided an example to the congregations around them. Members at Northwoods sensed that they might be in the forefront of a new way of being church. We often heard comments comparing themselves to other historically mainstream Protestant churches with a clear sense that *they* were not the ones "out of step."

At times, they ceased being the delicate objects of our study and we became the subject of their prophetic and pastoral ministries. As white males at Oakhurst, for example, we found ourselves confronted with our own collective and personal racism. At Cedar Grove we were challenged to put away professional pretensions and sophistication so that we might be genuinely present to people in the congregation. At Northwoods we were faced with a call to put our notebooks aside to participate in their quest to become multicultural. Such experiences turned the tables on us. We discovered depth in their strengths and at the same time became more aware of our own vulnerability, leading us to re-examine our vocations and assumptions as researchers.

Another line of reflection as we brought this study to conclusion led us back to our questions regarding why persons join, stay, or leave these congregations (these questions are explored in the fifth chapter). We continue to be impressed with the mystery involved in the decisions of people to participate in these congregations. We found no overt causal explanations for the remarkable transformations in the ways people related to people different from themselves and in the influence of these new ways of relating on their interpretations of what it means to live out of the good news of the gospel. We had a similar lack of explanation for the stories of resistance and rejection we heard from people (and about other people) who shared a similarly profound affection and loyalty to these congregations but could not imagine themselves in a church made up of people unlike themselves. People attribute the transformations in the lives of the former group to the spiritual vitality they experience in these congregations. The effects we saw are profound. Both pastors and laity often told us, for example, they could never again be a part of a congregation that did not embrace racial, cultural, and other forms of diversity. They enjoy too much participating in the creation of a church more consistent with their emerging image of God's love for all people. The mystery of these transformations was heightened for us as we pondered what prompted and sustained the radical changes in both some European Americans and in some African Americans as they moved out of historical patterns of racism and oppression to become enthusiastic members of congregations explicitly embracing cultural traditions originating in both Africa and Europe. In this regard they increasingly live out of assumptions alien to much of their daily experience. We find ourselves filled with wonder about the ways these congregations embody the simultaneous presence of fragility and vibrancy. Perhaps their experience of the persistent possibility of each points to a new way of being church in an era of radical and rapid social, economic, political, and religious change.

This study has not answered all of our questions about the impact of the dynamics of difference in congregational life. We were often asked, for example, "Is the pastor of any of these congregations black?" We soon discovered that the real question had to do with whether or not the pastor was black and male. We could say that the Barbadian youth minister of Northwoods had an African heritage. We also had to say that of historically Protestant mainline congregations embracing diversity of which we are aware, only Glide Church in San Francisco and The Riverside Church in New York have black male senior pastors. These answers did not satisfy those who questioned us. Further study is needed to sort out the local and systemic dynamics of racism, cultural privilege, class, power, gender, and cultural style at work in the recruitment, placement, and leadership of pastors of culturally diverse congregations.

We continue to wonder about the dichotomy we found in the denominational affirmation of the witness of these congregations and the simultaneous lack of any systemic strategy for fostering and supporting similar communities of faith. We would direct a similar query to theological schools, which in their own policies and curriculum seek to embrace diversity, yet continue to live out of models of education grounded in European cultural assumptions. Theological school rhetoric tends to affirm human diversity in church and community life, but academic programs do not focus on tasks integral to equipping students for leadership in contexts of diversity. In a sense we are not surprised that these institutional and systemic transformations have not occurred. Social responsivity to the power dynamics in the encounter of difference in its varied forms is very recent—especially in institutions. We may be in a time of social transformation—an era when the power dynamics in the diversity of human experience may be radically altered. Impetus to the possibilities of that transformation may most effectively derive from local practices and experience. Consequently, we find ourselves not so much lamenting the lack of social and systemic change directed to the embrace of difference at this point in human history as celebrating the willingness of members in these congregations to struggle for a vision of new ways of being in and creating Christian community. When we began this study we were intrigued by their counter-cultural embrace of diversity. As we conclude, we are grateful for their boldness in imaging what it means to be "church together" in the midst of the world's diversity and for their stubbornness, courage, and faithfulness in pursuing that vision.

Bibliography

Ammerman, Nancy Tatom. *Baptist Battles: Social Change and Religious Conflict in the Southern Baptist Convention.* New Brunswick: Rutgers University Press, 1990.

_____ . *Bible Believers: Fundamentalists in the Modern World.* New Brunswick: Rutgers University Press, 1987.

Apple, Michael W. *Ideology and Curriculum.* London: Routledge & Kegan Paul, 1979.

Aronowitz, Stanley, and Henry A. Giroux. *Postmodern Education: Politics, Culture, and Social Criticism.* Minneapolis: University of Minnesota Press, 1991.

Avery, Richard K., and Donald S. Marsh. "We Are the Church." In *The United Methodist Hymnal,* edited by Carlton R. Young, 558. Nashville: The United Methodist Publishing House, 1989.

Bailyn, Bernard. *Educational in the Forming of American Society: Needs and Opportunities for Study.* New York: Vintage Books, 1966.

Belenky, Mary Field, Blythe McVicker Clinchy, Nancy Rule Goldberger, Jill Mattuck Tarule. *Women's Ways of Knowing: The Development of Self, Voice, and Mind.* New York: Basic Books, 1986.

Bellah, Robert N. *Beyond Belief: Essays on Religion in a Post-Traditional World.* New York: Harper & Row, 1970.

Bellah, Robert N., Richard Madsen, William M. Sullivan, Ann Swidler, Steven M. Tipton. *Habits of the Heart: Individualism and Commitment in American Life.* Berkeley: University of California Press, 1985.

Berger, Peter L. *The Heretical Imperative: Contemporary Possibilities of Religious Affirmation.* Garden City, NY: Anchor Books, 1979.

Berger, Peter L., and Thomas Luckmann. *The Social Construction of Reality.* Garden City, NY: Doubleday, 1966 (reprinted by Anchor Books in 1990).

Bernstein, Richard J. *Beyond Objectivism and Relativism: Science, Hermeneutics, and Praxis.* Philadelphia: University of Pennsylvania Press, 1985.

Blakeney, Charles D., and Ronnie A. F. Blakeney. "Pluralism and the Dilemma of Discordance Among Blacks and Jews." In *The Challenge of Pluralism: Education, Politics and Values,* edited by F. Clark Power and Daniel K. Lapsley. Notre Dame, IN: University of Notre Dame Press, 1992.

Bowers, C. A. *Elements of a Post-Liberal Theory of Education.* New York: Teachers College Press, 1987.

Bowers, C. A., and David J. Flinders. *Responsive Teaching: An Ecological Approach to Classroom Patterns of Language, Culture, and Thought.* New York: Teachers College Press, 1990.

Boys, Mary C., ed. *Education for Citizenship and Discipleship.* New York: The Pilgrim Press, 1989.

Brown, Robert MacAfee. *Is Faith Obsolete?* Philadelphia: Westminster Press, 1974.

Brueggemann, Walter. *The Creative Word: Canon as a Model for Biblical Education.* Philadelphia: Fortress Press, 1982.

_____ . "The Legitimacy of a Sectarian Hermeneutic: 2 Kings 18-19." In *Education for Citizenship and Discipleship,* edited by Mary C. Boys. New York: The Pilgrim Press, 1989: 3-34.

_____ . *Texts Under Negotiation: The Bible and Postmodern Imagination.* Minneapolis: Fortress Press, 1993.

Bushnell, Horace. "Common Schools." In *Building Eras in Religion.* New York: Charles Scribner's Sons, 1881.

Cajete, Gregory. *Look to the Mountain: An Ecology of Indigenous Education.* Durango, CO: Kivaki Press, 1994.

Carroll, Jackson W., Carl S. Dudley, William McKinney. *Handbook for Congregational Studies.* Nashville: Abingdon Press, 1986.

Carter, Stephen L. *The Culture of Disbelief: How American Law and Politics Trivialize Religious Devotion.* New York: Basic Books, 1993.

Capers, William. *Catechism for Little Children: The Missions . . . of South Carolina.* Charleston: J.S. Burges, 1833.

Chopp, Rebecca. *The Power to Speak: Feminism, Language, God.* New York: The Crossroad Publishing Company, 1991.

Clark, David L. "Emerging Paradigms in Organizational Theory and Research." In *Organizational Theory and Inquiry: The Paradigm Revolution,* edited by Yvonna S. Lincoln. Beverly Hills: Sage Publications, 1985.

Coleman, John A. "Two Pedagogies: Discipleship and Citizenship." In *Education for Citizenship and Discipleship*, edited by Mary C. Boys. New York: The Pilgrim Press, 1989: 35-78.

Cremin, Lawrence A. *American Education: The National Experience 1783-1876*. New York: Harper Colophon Books, 1982.

_____. *Traditions of American Education*. New York: Basic Books, 1977.

Dewey, John. *Experience and Education*. New York: Collier Books, 1938.

Effective Christian Education: A National Study of Protestant Congregations. Minneapolis: Search Institute, 1990.

Eggleston, Edward. *The Transit of Civilization: From England to America in the Seventeenth Century*. Boston: Beacon Press, 1959 [1900].

Eisner, Elliott. *The Educational Imagination*. New York: Macmillan Publishing Co., 1979.

Elizondo, Virgilio. *Galilean Journey: The Mexican American Promise*. Maryknoll, NY: Orbis Books, 1983.

Epps, Edgar G., ed. *Cultural Pluralism*. Chicago: University of Chicago Press, 1974.

Erikson, Erik H. *Childhood and Society*. New York: Norton, 1962.

Foster, Charles R. "Communicating: Informal Conversation in the Congregation's Education." In *Congregations: Their Power to Form and Transform*, edited by C. Ellis Nelson. Richmond: John Knox Press, 1988: 218-37.

_____. "Double Messages: Ethnocentrism in the Education of the Church," *Religious Education* 82 (Summer 1987): 447-68.

_____. *Educating Congregations: The Future of Christian Education*. Nashville: Abingdon Press, 1994.

_____. *Ethnicity in the Education of the Church*. Nashville: Scarritt Press, 1987.

_____. "Imperialism in the Education of the Church," *Religious Education* 86 (Winter 1991): 145-56.

_____. *Teaching in the Community of Faith*. Nashville: Abingdon Press, 1982.

Foucault, Michel. *Power/Knowledge: Selected Interviews and Other Writings, 1972-1977*, edited by Colin Gordon. New York: Pantheon Books, 1980.

Fowler, James W. *Stages of Faith: The Psychology of Human Development and the Quest for Meaning*. San Francisco: Harper & Row, 1981.

Fraser, Nancy. *Unruly Practices: Power, Discourse and Gender in Contemporary Social Theory.* Minneapolis: University of Minnesota Press, 1989.

Freire, Paulo. *Pedagogy of the Oppressed.* New York: Continuum Publishing Company, 1986.

Geertz, Clifford. *The Interpretation of Cultures.* New York: Basic Books, 1973.

Gergen, Kenneth J. *The Saturated Self: Dilemmas of Identity in Contemporary Life.* New York: Basic Books, 1991.

Gerkin, Charles V. *The Living Human Document: Re-Visioning Pastoral Counseling in a Hermeneutical Mode.* Nashville: Abingdon Press, 1984.

Gilligan, Carol. *In a Different Voice: Psychological Theory and Women's Development.* Cambridge: Harvard University Press, 1982.

Giroux, Henry A. *Schooling and the Struggle for Public Life: Critical Pedagogy in the Modern Age.* Minneapolis: University of Minnesota Press, 1988.

_____ , ed. *Postmodernism, Feminism, and Cultural Politics: Redrawing Educational Boundaries.* Albany: State University of New York Press, 1991.

Giroux, Henry A., and Peter McLaren. *Between Borders: Pedagogy and the Politics of Cultural Studies.* New York: Routledge, 1994.

Greene, Maxine. *Landscapes of Learning.* New York: Teachers College Press, 1978.

Groome, Thomas H. *Christian Religious Education: Sharing our Story and Vision.* San Francisco: Harper & Row, 1980.

_____ . *Sharing Our Faith: A Comprehensive Approach to Religious Education and Pastoral Ministry.* HarperSanFrancisco, 1991.

Hale, Janice. *Black Children: Their Roots, Culture and Learning Styles.* Provo, UT: Brigham Young University Press, 1982.

_____ . *Unbank the Fire: Visions for the Education of African American Children.* Baltimore: Johns Hopkins University Press, 1994.

Haley, Alex. *Roots: The Saga of an American Family.* New York: Dell Publishing, 1976.

Hall, Edward T. *The Dance of Life: The Other Dimension of Time.* Garden City: Anchor/Doubleday, 1983.

_____ . *The Silent Language.* Greenwich, CT: Fawcett Publications, 1959.

Harris, Maria. *Fashion Me a People: Curriculum in the Church*. San Francisco: Harper & Row, 1989.

_____ . *Teaching and Religious Imagination*. New York: Harper & Row, 1987.

Herberg, Will. *Protestant, Catholic, Jew: An Essay in American Religious Sociology*. Garden City: Doubleday, 1955.

hooks, bell. *Teaching to Transgress: Education as the Practice of Freedom*. New York: Routledge, 1994.

_____ . *Yearning: Race, Gender, and Cultural Politics*. Boston: South End Press, 1990.

Hopewell, James F. *Congregations: Stories and Structures*. Philadelphia: Fortress Press, 1987.

Hutchison, William R. *Between the Times: The Travail of Protestant Establishment in America 1900-1960*. Cambridge: Cambridge University Press, 1989.

Kaufman, Gordon D. *In Face of Mystery: A Constructive Theology*. Cambridge: Harvard University Press, 1993.

Kegan, Robert. *In Over Our Heads: The Mental Demands of Modern Life*. Cambridge: Harvard University Press, 1994.

Kelly, Dean M. *Why Conservative Churches Are Growing: A Study in the Sociology of Religion*. New York: Harper & Row, 1972.

Kohlberg, Lawrence. *The Philosophy of Moral Development: Moral Stages and the Idea of Justice*. San Francisco: Harper & Row, 1981.

Kozol, Jonathan. *Savage Inequalities: Children in American Schools*. New York: Crown Publishers, 1991.

Lynn, Robert W. *Protestant Strategies of Education*. New York: Association Press, 1964.

Lynn, Robert W., and Elliot Wright. *The Big Little School: Two Hundred Years of the Sunday School*. Birmingham: Religious Education Press, 1980.

Marty, Martin E. *The Public Church: Mainline, Evangelical, Catholic*. New York: The Crossroad Publishing Co., 1981.

Matsuoka, Fumitaka. "Pluralism at Home: Globalization within North America." *Theological Education* XXVI (Spring 1990) Supplement I: 35-51.

McConnell, Taylor and June. *Family Ministry Through Cross-Cultural Education: A Final Report*. Evanston: The Leiffer Bureau of Social and Religious Research [Garrett-Evangelical Theological Seminary], 1990.

Moore, Allen J. "A Social Theory of Religious Education." In *Religious Education as Social Transformation*, edited by Allen

J. Moore. Birmingham: Religious Education Press, 1988.

Myers, William R. *Black and White Styles of Youth Ministry: Two Congregations in America*. New York: The Pilgrim Press, 1991.

Neibuhr, H. Richard. *The Meaning of Revelation*. New York: Macmillan Publishing Co., 1960.

Nelson, C. Ellis. *Where Faith Begins*. Richmond: John Knox Press, 1967.

Noddings, Nel. *Caring: A Feminine Approach to Ethics and Moral Education*. Berkeley: University of California Press, 1984.

Osmer, Richard Robert. *The Teachable Spirit: Recovering the Teaching Office in the Church*. Louisville: Westminster/John Knox Press, 1990.

Palmer, Parker. *To Know as We Are Known: A Spirituality of Education*. San Francisco: Harper & Row, 1983.

Peshkin, Alan. *The Color of Strangers, The Color of Friends: The Play of Ethnicity in School and Community*. Chicago: University of Chicago Press, 1991.

Pestalozzi, Heinrich. *How Gertrude Teaches Her Children: An Attempt to Help Mothers Teach Their Own Children and an Account of the Method*, edited by Ebenezer Cooke, translated by M. Joseph Costelle. New York: Ballantine Books, 1975 (1966).

Peterson, Anya Royce. *Ethnic Identity: Strategies of Diversity*. Bloomington: Indiana University Press, 1982.

Piaget, Jean. *The Development of Thought: Equilibration of Cognitive Structures*, translated by Arnold Rosin. New York: Viking Press, 1977.

Richardson, E. Allen. *Strangers in This Land: Pluralism and the Response to Diversity in the United States*. New York: The Pilgrim Press, 1988.

Riche, Martha Farnsworth. "We're All Minorities Now," *American Demographics* (October 1991): 26-91.

Ricoeur, Paul. *Hermeneutics and the Human Sciences: Essays on Language, Action, and Interpretation*, edited and translated by John B. Thompson. Cambridge: Cambridge University Press, 1981.

Rivers, Clarence Jos. "The Oral African Tradition Versus the Ocular Western Tradition." In *This Far by Faith: American Black Worship and Its African Roots*. Washington, DC: The National Office for Black Catholics and The Liturgical Conference, 1977.

Roof, Wade Clark, and William McKinney. *American Mainline Religion: Its Changing Shape and Future*. New Brunswick: Rutgers University Press, 1987.

Rorty, Richard. *Objectivity, Relativism and Truth: Philosophical Papers Volume I*. Cambridge: Cambridge University Press, 1991.

Russell, Letty M. *Church in the Round: Feminist Interpretation of the Church*. Louisville: Westminster/John Knox Press, 1993.

_____ . *The Future of Partnership*. Philadelphia: The Westminster Press, 1979.

_____ . *Growth in Partnership*. Philadelphia: The Westminster Press, 1981.

_____ . *Household of Freedom: Authority in Feminist Theology*. Philadelphia: The Westminster Press, 1987.

Safire, William. "Multi Multi-," in *The New York Times Magazine* (February 23, 1992): 20.

Sample, Tex. *U.S. Lifestyles and Mainline Churches: A Key to Reaching People in the 90's*. Louisville: Westminster/John Knox Press, 1990.

Schama, Simon. *Landscape and Memory*. New York: Alfred A. Knopf, 1995.

Schipani, Daniel J. *Religious Education Encounters Liberation Theology*. Birmingham: Religious Education Press, 1985.

Schreiter, Robert J. *Constructing Local Theologies*. Maryknoll, NY: Orbis Books, 1986.

Schüssler Fiorenza, Elizabeth. *Discipleship of Equals: A Critical Feminist Ekklesia-logy of Liberation*. New York: The Crossroad Publishing Company, 1993.

Shor, Ira. *Critical Teaching and Everyday Life*. Chicago: University of Chicago Press, 1980.

Sleeter, Christine E., and Carl A. Grant. "An Analysis of Multicultural Education in the United States," *Harvard Educational Review* 57 (November 1987): 421-44.

Stroupe, Gibson, and Inez Fleming. *While We Run This Race: Confronting the Power of Racism in a Southern Church*. Maryknoll, NY: Orbis Books, 1995.

Sugirtharajah, R. S. *Voices from the Margin: Interpreting the Bible in the Third World*. Maryknoll, NY: Orbis Books, 1991.

Turner, Victor. *The Ritual Process: Structure and Anti-Structure* Ithaca, NY: Cornell Paperbacks, 1969.

Wagner, C. Peter. *Our Kind of People: The Ethical Dimensions of Church Growth in America*. Atlanta: John Knox Press, 1979.

Warner, Stephen R. *New Wine in Old Wineskins: Evangelicals and Liberals in a Small-town Church*. Berkeley: University of California Press, 1988.

Welch, Sharon. *Communities of Resistance and Solidarity: A Feminist Theology of Liberation*. Maryknoll, NY: Orbis Books, 1985.

_____ . "An Ethic of Solidarity and Difference." In *Postmodernism, Feminism, and Cultural Politics: Redrawing Educational Boundaries*, edited by Henry A. Giroux. Albany: State University of New York Press, 1991: 83-99.

_____ . *A Feminist Ethic of Risk*. Minneapolis: Fortress Press, 1990.

Westerhoff, John H. III. *Values for Tomorrow's Children: An Alternative Future for Education in the Church*. Philadelphia: The Pilgrim Press, 1970.

Wheatley, Margaret. *Leadership and the New Science: Learning About Organization from an Orderly Universe*. San Francisco: Berrett-Loehler, 1992.

Williams, Colin W. *Where in the World? Changing Forms of the Church's Witness*. New York: National Council of the Churches of Christ in the U.S.A., 1963.

Wind, James P., and James W. Lewis. *American Congregations*. Chicago: University of Chicago Press, 1994; II.

Wuthnow, Robert. *The Struggle for America's Soul: Evangelicals, Liberals, and Secularism*. Grand Rapids: Eerdmans Publishing Co., 1989.

Young, Iris Marion. *Justice and the Politics of Difference*. Princeton: Princeton University Press, 1990.

Index